T0003282

CONFESSIONS OF A
CAFETERIA CATHOLIC

PETER J. KREEFT
and
NAT WHILK

Confessions of a
Cafeteria Catholic

IGNATIUS PRESS   SAN FRANCISCO

Cover art and design
by Enrique J. Aguilar

© 2022 by Ignatius Press, San Francisco
All rights reserved
ISBN 978-1-62164-481-1 (PB)
ISBN 978-1-64229-201-5 (eBook)
Library of Congress Control Number 2021940708
Printed in the United States of America ⊗

Contents

Introduction

by Peter Kreeft

"Introduction" means literally "leading into". Somebody leads somebody into something.

The "somebody" who is leading here is me, of course; and the "somebody" whom I am trying to lead is you, the reader; and the "something" into which I am here trying to lead is this book.

It is a strange book. First, because it is a series of letters. Second, because I didn't write it all. Nat Whilk wrote the first part of this book, the single short article "Confessions of a Cafeteria Catholic". He also chose the title; I stole it from him. Nat self-labels that way; I do not. He is the "cafeteria Catholic", and I am the "eat all the food Mommy puts on your plate" Catholic.

The longest part of this book was originally one long personal letter from me to Nat, in response to that short article of his. I split it up into twenty shorter parts, like a mommy cutting up baby's meat for easier consumption. (Don't feel insulted; we are all babies. Did you really think you were an "adult"? Do you frequent "adult" movies and bookstores? Do you defend "adult-ery"?)

"Nat" is a pen name, a pseudonym. I know who Nat is, but I won't tell, not even whether Nat is male (Nathan) or female (Natalie). After I read Nat's article (which is the first part of this book), I asked him for his permission to publish it along with my long response, which is the second part of this book, and his response to my response (the third part) and my response to his response to my response (the fourth part). We are both trying to prove we are very response-able.

I call Nat "him", not to reveal his gender, but because my publisher and I still use traditional inclusive-language pronouns. If you don't like this tradition, I have four questions for you. (If you find the issue tedious, you have my congratulations and my permission to skip the next four paragraphs.)

1. Would you really want me to be "politically correct" and say: "I asked him or her for his or her permission to write him or her a long response . . . and he or she graciously gave me his or her permission to publish his or her two letters"? I do not think that the best way to atone for old sins against women is by inventing new sins against language.

2. Why do they call the old *in*clusive use of "he" to refer equally to males and females "*ex*clusive" and why do they call the new "politically correct" language "*in*clusive" when it deliberately *ex*cludes females from this old, traditionally inclusive pronoun?

3. Why do they insist that the real hidden and sinister purpose of the old inclusive language was to exclude females if almost none of the writers who used that old language meant to do that? Are they claiming to psychoanalyze millions of dead writers and accusing them all of self-deception or lying? I am on Shakespeare's side even if he is dead.

4. What is your response to the following joke about "pronoun wars"? At Harvard Divinity School, the "politically correct" experts insisted on changing the traditional pronoun referring to God from "he" to "he or she". And

then the feminists pointed out that "he" still came first, so they changed it to "she or he". And then the earth-first people and the tree-huggers and the Gaia worshippers and the New Agers protested that "it" was excluded, so they changed it to "she or he or it". That was too long, so they condensed it to one syllable. Did you find that funny or unfunny? *Why?*

These four questions are a test of your level of "political correctness". If you did not laugh at all, you get an A for Adamant. If you laughed but felt guilty about it, you get a C for Conflicted. If you laughed without guilt, you get an F for Fun-loving. I thank God for humorless humans; they give us something to laugh at.

This book is personal, one-to-one, I-to-Thou. The reason I am publicly publishing my reply to Nat is because I want to talk to you, privately, and to many other Nats, other "cafeteria Catholics". But I want this book to be a personal letter to you, dear reader, rather than an impersonal "publication" addressed to "the public". I have never met "the public", and I strongly suspect that it is a ghost. I don't talk to ghosts.

If you identify with all or part of Nat's stance toward the most controversial institution that ever existed, namely, the Catholic Church;

If, after some independent and personal "critical thinking" on your part, you find that you have some love and loyalty toward her (enough to classify yourself as at least some sort of Catholic), but that you disagree with some of her official teachings, for which she claims to have divine, not just human, authority;

If you think that this large Thing is somewhere between being God's holy and beautiful bride and being the Devil's unholy, horrible whore, something neither infallibly wrong nor infallibly right;

If, in other words, if you, like Nat, are a "cafeteria Catholic", then this letter is intended for you, too, just as much and just as personally as it was for Nat.

If you are *not* a "cafeteria Catholic", either because you are less Catholic than that or more Catholic than that, you are still invited to be a fly on the wall and listen in, because the issues about which Nat and I argue are very important, very controversial, and therefore very interesting.

And also because "cafeteria Catholics" and ex-Catholics together make up the single largest religious identity group in America. So even if you are not in this large group yourself, you almost certainly have friends who are. And there is no real friendship without conversation. Here is a contribution to that conversation.

~

The twenty numbered parts of my response to Nat look like the twenty chapters in the Table of Contents of a book, but they are really my answers to each of the twenty paragraphs in Nat's letter. I added the twenty numbers to his letter, in the order Nat wrote his paragraphs, because Nat and I both tend to be very orderly thinkers, and the simplest kind of order is a numbered list. Please reread each of Nat's numbered paragraphs before reading my answers to it.

Please keep in mind that this book is a personal letter, not an academic treatise or textbook, whether in theology or philosophy or psychology or sociology. It has the repetitions and meanderings of any real letter to a real person because it is personal and spontaneous and from the heart. It is an I-Thou, not an I-It, relationship.

PART ONE

"Confessions of a Cafeteria Catholic"

by Nat Whilk

I have been accused of being a "cafeteria Catholic" by many of my Catholic friends who still faithfully believe and try to practice everything their Church teaches, who eat everything Mother Church puts on their plate, even the vegetables. I do not. Here is my defense.

I do not find the term "cafeteria Catholic" an insult but a compliment. For although I am not a genius or a saint—or a professional theologian—I am an adult with a free will, a personal conscience, and a questioning, critical mind. And when I turn these three powers of my soul upon the Catholic Church, I find in that institution both much to accept and even love and also much to refuse and even despise. As does most of the rest of the world, I think—not only those outside of the Catholic Church, but also many who are to some degree or other "in" her. I therefore write this article as a kind of manifesto, and I address it to "the True Believer", or the "non-cafeteria Catholic".

1. To me, the overarching question is about authority. I do not see authority as the best way to find the truth, as the True Believer does. The average "True Believer" or "non-cafeteria Catholic" accepts everything Mother Church gives him, *not* because he has personally examined and evaluated each of the tenets and dogmas and claims and commandments of this religion, one by one, by his own reasoning, but by "faith", which means trust in authority.

That is not just my definition of faith but also that of the "True Believer". In fact, the old "Baltimore Catechism" defined faith that way, in terms of authority: "Faith is an act of the intellect, prompted by the will, by which we believe everything God has revealed on the grounds of the authority of the One who has revealed it [Who can neither deceive nor be deceived]."

So the Catechism is saying that faith is like a chain with

three links: God, the Church, and me. The Church is the middle link, the mediator, God's authoritative prophet to us. I have no problems with God or His infallibility, nor with myself and my fallibility; but I do have problems with the middle link in the chain, which is the Church. It seems to me naïve and childish to identify that middle link in the chain with God and His infallibility rather than with us and our fallibility. The Church looks much, much more human than divine to me.

2. If you insist on tying God to the Church, you will make me an atheist. That is like gluing the Hope Diamond to the back of a wild rhinoceros and telling me I have to take it or leave it as a package deal. If the Church is what God looks like, I am not buying that package. I cannot ride that animal.

And if you ask me to check my critical reason at the church door and simply accept it all by trusting its "authority", you are asking me to be a slave and to let the Church be my master. To be a critical thinker is by definition to pick and choose, as in a cafeteria. I insist on applying even to the Church the advice Saint Paul gives: "Test all things; hold fast to that which is good." The testing is critical reason; the holding fast is religious faith. I want faith, too, but I want to base my faith on reason, not authority; on right rather than might.

3. Why, then, do I call myself a Catholic? Because I love most of the food they serve in this cafeteria. As I said, I have no problems with God, and the Catholic Church is the biggest "God business" in the world. She does the world's best job in cultivating a sense of mystery and wonder and transcendence that is far from fundamentalist literalism but also far from atheism, which I find empty and arid and cold, like outer space. Her theology is an unparalled work of art.

Her God is much more than The Guy in the Sky or Santa Claus for Adults. Ned Flanders, meet Thomas Aquinas and take some philosophy lessons.

Best of all, her God is Love. The Church does not always *act* as if that is true, but she *teaches* it, at least. And that is absolutely central. I suspect that deep down all of us, even atheists and agnostics, know that that love is the absolute, the ultimate value, the meaning of life. If it turns out that "God" is only a personification of love, I can live with that; but I cannot live with a God who is judgmental and self-righteous and arrogant and angry, like so many who claim to be His representatives.

4. If you love someone, you respect his freedom and unique individuality. If you hate or despise or fear others, you try to crush their freedom. The Church's historical track record here is worse than spotty. Once she emerged from the catacombs and the persecutions and the lions in the Coliseum, once Constantine became the first Christian emperor, once the Church got political power, the two sides switched positions: she became the new Roman Empire, and heretics became the new martyrs.

The Church no longer burns heretics at the stake today, partly because nobody cares enough about theology to do that anymore. But we still care about morality, and the stakes are still pretty high and hot for feminists, gays, lesbians, transgenders, divorcees, pro-choicers, contracepters, aborters, adulterers, fornicators, masturbaters, and lusters. The polls show that most Catholics as well as non-Catholics think that trying to wear the whole of Catholic morality as a one-size-fits-all uniform feels like trying to wear a suit of medieval armor complete with a "chastity belt". It doesn't fit any more. The Middle Ages are over. (Call out the reporters!) We need a suit that fits what we actually are.

The song that threatens the Church's authority the most is Sinatra's "I Did It My Way". Paul Newman once made a movie about euthanasia with the title "Whose Life Is It, Anyway?" Dictators answer that question by saying "It's mine". Lovers answer it by saying to each other "It's yours". If you love me, you must love my freedom. Love, in contrast to law, has to be free. The Bible says God is love. It does not say God is law.

5. Criticizing the Church for no longer making moral clothes that are fit for us to wear raises the great question: What are we? What is it to be a human being today? And what is it to be a human being in any age?

Some say that "biology is destiny". (They are Materialists.) Others say that predestination is destiny. (They are Calvinists.) I say that freedom is destiny.

Human beings are the only beings we know of in the universe that freely choose their own values, their own meaning, their own identity. God and/or nature gives us our raw material, "what" we are; but we shape it by our free choices into "who" we are. And that freedom is sacred. Our nature does not determine our freedom. Our freedom determines our nature. In giving us free choice, God gave us the power to co-create ourselves, to shape ourselves, to determine what kind of person we will be. The Church, with her one-size-fits-all "natural law" morality, has a lot of respect for our impersonal universal human nature, for "what" we are, but not much respect for our individual human freedom, for "who" we are.

America is a great country because it is a democracy. The Catholic Church is not as great a church as she should be because she is not a democracy.

6. At the heart of freedom is moral freedom of conscience. Here again, the Church fails to practice what she

preaches. She preaches the profound principle that it is always a sin to violate your own individual, private, personal conscience. Yet she imposes upon our personal conscience a massive set of impersonal, universal, no-exceptions answers to a host of complex moral questions: answers from which she does not leave us free to dissent.

Her "natural law morality" treats values—*her* values—as if they were facts. That is not only a moral mistake (disrespecting freedom) but also a logical mistake, a category confusion. "Is" does not entail "ought". The morality of "natural law" puts more in its conclusion (the "ought") than it has in its premises (the "is"). "Nature" is the sum total of all facts, "ises". "Laws" are moral values or duties, "oughts". "Nature" is fact, "law" is value; "nature" is what is, law is what ought to be. So the very term "natural law" is an oxymoron. It confuses and identifies those two opposite things.

7. The most intimate, impassioned, and important aspects of our lives almost always have something to do with our sexuality. And it is here that the Church shows her instinct for authoritarian dictatorship most clearly. She is obsessed with "pelvic issues". Even Pope Francis told us to "stop obsessing about abortion". The Church will not listen to the vast majority of voices from her own laity and clergy and theologians who see contraception, abortion, same-sex attraction, and sexual activity outside of marriage as things (facts, practices, activities) that can be used for either good or evil. This, again, is the one-size-fits-all morality that the Church calls the "natural law" but that is really unnatural legal*ism*.

8. The priestly pedophilia scandals testify to how unsuccessful this focus on sex has been for the Church. It simply has not worked, in the real world. Actions not only

speak louder than words but speak a word of their own. The Church has lost her moral credibility. She herself cannot practice what she preaches.

I am not, of course, advocating tolerating sexual predators. I am advocating a kind of relaxation and trusting confidence in human freedom to replace a rigid, absolutistic, perfectionistic, puritanical, guilt-inducing legalism. And that includes allowing priests to marry and women to be ordained.

9. This obsession with sex is especially evident in the Church's simplistic and total No to contraception. Almost 90 percent of American Catholics disagree, both in belief and in practice. In the face of nearly unanimous dissent based on the massive experience of the laity , that "no" by a few celibates is simply ridiculous and unlivable, beyond the pale of argument. *Humanae Vitae* was the Church's Waterloo.

10. The Church is also obsessed with a simplistic, no-compromise attitude to abortion. But compromise is possible. Moses was pro-choice. He loved both life and free choice, so he said, "*Choose* life". The Church has forgotten the first half of that sentence.

11. The Church should concentrate on social justice and peace, and on political issues that affect the whole community, instead of obsessing about private, individual issues, especially sexual issues. That is not what Jesus and all the prophets did. Compare how much they talked about sex with how much they talked about money.

12. Insofar as the Church has addressed social and political issues, throughout most of her past history she has made the disastrous mistake, both in her teaching and in her practice, of defending both "throne and altar", Church and State, the "ancient regime" of both political and religious hierarchy, authority, and obedience: "the establishment". Only recently and reluctantly has she begun to embrace modern

values like freedom, equality, democracy, consensus, pluralism, tolerance, nonjudgmentalism, and the separation of Church and State. Deep down, the Church is still nostalgic about the Middle Ages, when she had all the power, over the secular as well as the sacred. The corruption that that alliance produced was notorious (Inquisitions, Crusades), and we still live with its echoes.

13. Scientific as well as political revolutions are what defined modernity, and to both kinds of revolution the Church has been the drag factor if not the outright enemy. She has never come to terms with science and the Enlightenment, with intellectual adulthood, with "man come of age". Her first, instinctive reaction to every technological advancement, especially in the life sciences, is suspicion and fear. She is living in the past and still fighting the wars of science and religion. But science keeps advancing, and religion keeps retreating throughout the world. It is naïve to ignore the causal relationship between those two lines on the graph. The more science has succeeded, the more religion has failed. It is time to end the war and make friends with our "enemy", for the sake of sheer survival.

14. "Science" does not mean "materialism". Science has no more disproved the existence of God or the spiritual soul than it has proved them. I do not defend materialism, either in theory (for we are not soulless machines) or in practice (for the meaning of life is not consumerism). What I have a quarrel with is not spirituality but authoritarianism, not religion but organized religion, not religious communities but the institutional Church. Religion has done great good (saints, hospitals, social justice) but also great evils (witch hunts, inquisitions, crusades, heresy hunting). Like everything human, it is two-faced. But it does not admit that and absurdly claims to be "infallible" and "holy". God's reaction

to that claim has to be Psalm 2:4: "He who sits in the heavens laughs; the LORD has them in derision." The Church claims that it is "the kingdom of God" but Jesus said, "The kingdom of God is within you" (Lk 17:21 KJV).

15. We see in the New Testament this constant conflict between Jesus and the official representatives of the religious institution. Cynical, power-hungry, egotistic, hypocritical, judgmental, legalistic, ritualistic, superstitious—the Pharisees are not a dead ancient Jewish sect but a live modern Catholic mind-set. I say an unequivocal Yes to Jesus; that is why I do not say an unequivocal Yes to the Church. Jesus was "the man for others", but the Church wants to package Him as her own private product. She wants to corner the Jesus market.

The Church has a good product to sell. The Mass is a beautiful ritual. But honestly, I usually get more spiritual benefit from a Quaker silent meeting, from Buddhist meditation, from Hindu yoga, or from a walk in the woods. Groups that the Church labels heretical seem to me much closer to Jesus, to the spirit of Christ, than Catholics: Quakers, Unitarians, Mormons, and so-called "modernists". The fewer creeds and commandments they have, the more love they seem to have.

So I want to be all of these things as well as Catholic. I want it all. I want both/and instead of either/or. Religion itself is a cafeteria, and I want the right to concoct my own supper by taking what I find valuable from many parts of that big restaurant.

16. Why, then, do I call myself a Catholic if I am so eclectic? My answer is that I respect all religions, but the Catholic one is the one I was born into: it's like my family. I do not claim that my family is the only good family or the

absolutely best one in the world. But that does not prevent me from being loyal to it.

Surely there are many roads up the religious mountain. What matters is not the horizontal dimension (which road are we on?) but the vertical dimensions (are we rising toward God on our road?). We should be tolerant and respectful of the roads, except for the one that is intolerant and disrespectful of all the others.

17. I still call myself a Catholic because I find many things I love inside my Church as well as outside, i.e., the many good works she has performed throughout history. I would miss her enormously if she folded up shop. All the landmarks of life—birth, baptism, coming-of-age, sickness, guilt, marriage, funerals—are touched by her sacraments. I do not believe I have to sign every line of an arcane and ancient creed in order to receive them.

18. I was baptized in a church, married in a church, continue occasionally to receive communion in a church, and hope to have my life commemorated at a funeral in a church. The Church, like the Sabbath, was made for man, not man for her. Jesus got it right.

19. "Catholic" means "universal". I only ask the Church to live up to her name and enlarge her big tent, to exchange her exclusivism for inclusivism, her fanaticism for tolerance, her narrowness for broadness.

Here is my favorite Catholic joke: "We Catholics are very broad and tolerant. We say to everyone: You worship God in your own way, and we'll worship Him in His."

20. Meanwhile, I will continue to work to reform and update this great institution, to do my small part to help to bring to birth a renewed Church that can serve the real world.

PART TWO

Response

by Peter Kreeft

Introduction

(My Response to the First Two Unnumbered Paragraphs of Nat's Article)

Dear Nat,

I am one of those "non-cafeteria Catholics" to whom you have addressed your letter, which you call a kind of "manifesto of a cafeteria Catholic". I assume that you were serious, so I read your letter seriously, as a fair and honest challenge, and here is my response.

I am convinced that both your letter and you are very worth responding to. Your letter, because it hits all the most important controversial issues in a very clear, direct, simple, and logical way. You, because you seem not only intelligent but also honest and passionate, and I respect and admire many things about your head (your logical reasoning) and even more about your heart (your loving motives).

Your letter is like a good story: it is connected. Each point flows from the one before it and into the one after it like the events of a narrative plot, like the steps of an escalator, or like a row of dominoes. Yet though they are logically related, they are also distinct, so that both your arguments and mine can be ordered, one by one, like the many different

27

courses of an epicure's dinner, not all mixed up and messed up together like a shake in a blender.

When I was younger, I agreed with pretty much everything you say in your letter. I was not, like you, born and raised as a Catholic, so I knew only what most semi-educated people know about Catholicism, and I naturally found many of those things appealing and others unappealing, as one would probably find the strange foods in a large foreign cafeteria. But when I tried to think seriously through these issues (the many issues that divide Catholics from non-Catholics), I saw one thing more and more clearly, long before I became convinced that the Catholic positions were all true: I saw that they were all part of a package deal; that they were, indeed, like dominoes in a chain or steps on an escalator or events in a narrative. To put it in another image that you will probably not like very much because it pictures the Church in a rather authoritarian and non-egalitarian way, I saw that the Church was not like a cafeteria for food shoppers but like a high chair for babies: to be a Catholic, you had to accept all the food Mommy put on your plate. She was Mommy; she was very much older and wiser than you; she had *authority*.

So I agree with your first point: that the Church's "authoritarianism" is her first and fundamental problem. And like you, I thought that was an insult to our intelligence and freedom. If the Church is our Mother, that makes us babies.

And much of the food in this cafeteria did not look edible; the cooks did not look trustable; and the waitstaff did not look clean and spiffy. Catholics often identify the Church with Noah's ark. Their point is that she is "the ark of salvation", that she saves you from the flood, from death, from eternal death; that she saves souls as Noah's Ark saved bodies. As a non-Catholic, I certainly did not believe that. But

I thought that image was well chosen, because the Church did, indeed, look like Noah's Ark in many other ways: she looks like an amateur rather than a professional job, hand-made, slow and laborious; she held every species of smelly, unruly animals and tons of animal poop; and she was manned by a small coterie of inexperienced, incompetent, confused sailors who knew next to nothing about sailing. The fact that the storms of history had not sunk that leaky old tub was miraculous.

Like you, I was impressed by the sophisticated philosophy of her theologians (like Aquinas) and by the high morality of her saints; and, like you, I was impressed by the contrast between the high morality the Church taught and the low morality by which most of her members and even many of her clergy lived, both in the past (e.g., the spectacularly cor-rupt Borgia popes) and recent times (e.g., pedophile priests). I was also impressed (i.e., impressively unimpressed) by her boringly blasé catechism classes (so boring that they were almost interesting, like a pile of mud a mile high) and her "Catholic" universities that were embarrassed at their name and the burden of their heritage. My obvious question then was: If her teachings were "winners", why were her teach-ers such "losers"?

Any merely human business that incompetent would not last two generations. Why had she lasted for eighty gen-erations? Why is she still alive? Is it simply because there are billions of naïve idiots and suckers in the world? Were Augustine and Aquinas and Saint Francis and Pascal and Shakespeare and Newman and Chesterton and Tolkien and Mother Teresa all idiots and suckers? She claims to be a prophet, and she looks like a prostitute, but she is certainly a puzzle. She claims to be holy and looks to be whorey, but she certainly is hoary, the oldest institution on earth: not just a Mother, but a great-great-grandmother. Why hasn't Grandma died, like everybody else?

Why some intelligent people still believe her may be a puzzle, but why some intelligent people do *not* believe her is no puzzle. You have identified twenty of her apparently inedible foods that she offers us. That is why you are a "cafeteria Catholic". In this long letter, I will try to explain why all the bad-tasting spinach Mother Church puts on our plate is good food. I certainly do not expect you to say instantly "Oh! I see!" and convert or revert when you read this book. But I do think I see the answers. Because I do see the questions. For I was once almost exactly where you are.

1. Authority

Nat, you have hit the nail on the head. The overarching issue is authority. You are right: Catholics have not figured out all these Catholic teachings by themselves, by their own reason, but have accepted them by faith: that is to say that they have accepted all the stuff Mother Church gives them because they trust her authority, as children trust their parents and students trust their teachers.

But that is how *all* religion works. Muslims trust the authority of the Qur'an. Hindus trust the authority of their mystics and gurus. Buddhists trust the authority of Buddha, or of his "enlightenment" experience. Jews trust the authority of their tradition, "the Law and the Prophets". If you had figured it all out for yourself, you would not buy into *any* religion; you would make your own. That is the difference between religion and science. Science rightly discounts faith and trust and authority. That is the first step of the scientific method: universal methodic doubt. Premodern scientists made many mistakes because they confused the method of science with the method of religion. They used a kind of religious faith and trust and reverence for great ancient scientists like Aristotle. Today, we are making exactly the same mistake in the opposite direction: demanding a scientific attitude to religion instead of a religious attitude toward science. Is it so unreasonable to ask for a scientific attitude toward science and a religious attitude toward religion instead? Do we trust mathematicians to explain and judge love poems or romantic lovers to judge mathematical equations? Do we ask serious scholars to write about humor? In my own field, philosophy, I am thinking of writing a funny book about humor because there are none: they are all deadly dull and serious.

That does *not* mean I advocate checking your mind at the church door. It just means not thinking that the scientific method will determine whether or not that thing that looks like a little round piece of bread to the eyes and to the microscope is really not what it appears to be but is the Body of Christ because God is performing a miracle there. That may be a profound truth, or it may be a ridiculous superstition, but science can neither prove it nor disprove it. If you say science disproves it, that would be like saying that not finding God in a test tube proves atheism. That would be like saying that religion disproves quantum theory because you can't find it in the Bible. It confuses two different things, two different methods. The point is simply that there are many methods, many ways of thinking rightly, and math and science are not the only ones. The human mind is bigger than that.

The idea that faith goes beyond reason does not mean that we do not need to give reasons for faith. It means that there is more than one way of finding truth. The scientific method is one way, but faith in some authority is another, and common sense, as summarized in tradition, is a third, and good philosophical reasoning is a fourth. If you believe that the scientific method is the only way of finding or proving truth, then you must believe that before the rise of the scientific method, no one ever found or proved any truth about anything.

Most of what we believe, we believe because we trust

the relevant authorities: that Antarctica is cold and getting warmer; that Mozart's music is beautiful; that love is good; that $E=MC^2$; that the people you think are your parents are really your parents; and that war is a really bad way to solve disputes. It is just as inappropriate to ask a scientist whether God loves us as it is to ask a priest what quasars are.

You are right in rejecting thoughtless authoritarianism. We ought to have good reasons for trusting authorities, in every field. But reason often does lead us to trust authorities in religion. There is a whole enterprise, called "apologetics", devoted to that: giving reasons for faith, i.e., for trust in the authority of God, of Christ, and of Christ's Church. I am not assuming that the enterprise of apologetics succeeds, I am just noting that the enterprise exists and ought to exist. There is also, and ought to be, an atheistic apologetics enterprise, and a Protestant one, and a Muslim one. It is just as wrong to *dismiss* authority without reason as it is to *accept* it without reason. "Come, let us reason together." That is what I hope we are doing in this correspondence.

"Authority" is maligned today because it is usually misunderstood. Most people think it means force, or power to enforce; that it means that "might makes right". It is exactly the opposite: authority is not the right of might but the might of right. The word "authority" has the word "author" in it. It means "author's rights". If God is our "author", the Creator and Designer of our nature and our life, then He has the same kind of natural, inherent right to tell us what we are and why we exist as the human author of an invention or of a novel has to label the invention or the characters he designed and to say what their meaning and purpose are. That is not a proof that God exists, but it is a defense of the reasonableness of the concept of divine authority: if the Creator God exists, He has an authority over us that we do not have over Him. If, on the other hand, God is our invention rather than we His, then we have authority over Him just as we do over Santa Claus. Assuming either one of those two things, atheism or theism, from the get-go, so that you don't have to give reasons for it, makes reasonable dialogue impossible.

I don't claim that this is a proof or even an argument for believing that God exists or that there is such a thing as divine authority. But I do claim that it is an explanation of the rationality of belief in God *and* in authority as a logically consistent "package deal". I do not see how you can believe in God without believing He has the same kind of natural authority over us as we have over our inventions or our art. But I don't believe He has the kind of tyrannical authority that says "Don't think for yourself, just pray, pay, and obey."

Even subhuman things have a lesser kind of natural authority over us simply by having their own nature independent of us and our thought. Dogs and trees and rocks do not have human rights, of course, but they have the right to be recognized as what they are; they have the authority of truth over our minds. We are *wrong*, we are stupid, if we treat dogs like trees or confuse trees with rocks. Science would be impossible without that "authority" of reality, or of objective truth, over our minds.

If we begin with this most generic authority, the authority of objective truth, the next question is whether "God exists" is an objective truth. We need good reasons for answering either Yes or No to that question. If the answer is Yes, the next question is whether Jesus is who he claims to be, the divine Son of God, with divine authority. If the answer is Yes again, the next question is whether the Catholic Church is what she claims to be, the authoritative voice of the Son of God. If she is, then Catholics are right in accepting the Church's authority, and "cafeteria Catholicism" is the same kind of mistake as saying that Jesus was right on Sunday but not on Monday or that God was right to issue eight of the Commandments but not the other two.

The point is that we have to be logically consistent. At each stage of the argument, we are intellectually and morally obligated to obey the command of the first pope. Saint Peter, who tells us to "be prepared to make a defense . . . for the hope that is in you" (1 Pet 3:15). I quite agree with your principle here.

Not only is it false that "might makes right", but the very reverse is true in a way: that "right makes might". Being right makes its own kind of might, a kind of might or power that is spiritual, not physical or financial or social sanction or pressure or fear of punishment. There is a Chinese word for it, *te*, which means the spiritual power of truth and goodness and beauty to attract and convince and convert the human soul. This spiritual force is very different from physical forces or even external social forces such as laws and sanctions. It works, not to constrict free choice, but to perfect free choice, to enlighten and inform free choice, as the mind influences and benefits the will, as a ship's navigator influences and benefits the captain. It is what Aristotle would call a formal cause rather than an efficient cause. It is not a deterministic cause, like dominoes pushing each other down, but a personal and spiritual "influence", like the influx of light onto a colored surface. To use a spatial metaphor, it comes vertically, from above, like sunlight, not horizontally, like billiard balls on a table.

This is just common sense. We all accept this kind of authority every day, when we believe the news, our textbooks, our friends, or even our own senses (since we *can* doubt them). Ninety-nine percent of what we know, we know because we trust authorities. These authorities are not infallible, so we need to think critically about them. We need to have reasons for trusting our authorities. Honest, humble, and open-minded agnostics do begin there, with an acknowledgment of our own ignorance and need. No one, in fact, begins by innately knowing whether or not God is real or whether or not Christ is God or whether or not the Church's dogmas are infallible, as we know innately that we exist and that $2+2=4$. So we all need to think about these important questions "critically". The word means, not necessarily "negatively", but "rationally and open-mindedly". I know you know that, but many people do not. They think that only skepticism and debunking is "critical" and free and rational thinking, and that acceptance and admiration are naïve, unclever, and unfree.

"Critical thinking" is what we two are doing right now about the Church. Both of us have thought about it, and you have come to the conclusion that the Church does not have the authority she claims to have, and I have come to the conclusion that she does. That's why you are a "cafeteria Catholic" and I am not. Both of us have reasons for our different beliefs. That's the question that divides us, not the question of whether we should accept "authority" at all or in general. You do not reject authority in general and as such. No one can in fact do that, though he can think he is doing it. And I do not accept all authority, as you seem to think I do. In fact, it was a cliché among medieval philosophers that the argument from merely human authority is the weakest of all arguments. Medieval philosophers were truly critical thinkers.

In any case, we two are not most fundamentally arguing

about authority, we are arguing about the Church, about what she is. Authority is merely one possible reason for choosing to believe something to be true. It is a means to the desired end of knowing what is. I insist that we need to have good *reasons* for trusting authority, and I hope you do, too, because that means that you agree that sometimes we *should* trust an authority. So I think that the issue that divides us is, first of all, not the method (authority vs. reason), but the truth: Is the Church really what she claims to be, the voice with divine authority, or not?

I believe there is a relationship, a kind of chain, between the objective truth and our subjective minds, and three of the links in that chain are God, Christ, and the Church, in that order. For atheists, God is the weak link in the chain, because He is a myth, not a truth at all. For Jews and Muslims, it is Christ who is the weak link, because according to them He is not the God I think He is. For you, it is the Church that is the weak link, because for you she is not the authoritative voice of the divine Christ whom you love and in whom believe as I also do. There is a theological term for you. You are a Protestant.

I trust you also understand that the Church's view of authority is nuanced and leveled. She claims infallible authority only for her dogmas of theology or morality that she claims are divinely revealed. These are relatively few, and they are always clearly labeled. They have one of two verbal formulas to identify them: either "ex cathedra", which means "from the chair of Peter as the first pope, and with the authority Christ gave to Peter", or the Vincentian formula, "which has been believed by all Christians in all times and places" from the beginning, or "by the authority given by Christ and His apostles". Absent these formulae, there is still authority, and an authority that makes rightful claims on us; but it is like the authority of a human parent in that it is not claimed to be absolutely infallible and unchangeable.

Once I say "not infallible", you probably naturally think, "not authoritative". That is a misunderstanding. We have lost the concept of an authority that is less than infallible yet more than an ideal or a recommendation or a suggestion and more than mere might; an authority that has *te*, or moral force, yet is not infallible.

Why are we so suspicious of authority? Probably because the practical consequence of accepting an authority is "trust and obey", or "obey because you trust". We had that trust toward our parents when we were small, and we had it toward prophets, priests, and kings, toward seers, saints, and sages, when the human race was young. We probably overdid it then, and we probably underdo it now. Once we were little kids, but we at least knew who we were. Now, we are teenagers who think we are adults. Once, we divinized the fallible human authority of our fathers on earth. Now, we have humanized the infallible authority of our Father in Heaven.

But our question, Nat, is simpler than all that global and historical pop psychology. It is this: If we believe in God and in Jesus Christ as His divine Son incarnate, and in their rightful authority over us, is that authority exercised over us through the Catholic Church or not? Is the Church the rightful inheritor of His authority, or is she an illegitimate pretender to it?

2. God

Our image of the chain with three links—God, Christ, Church—allows me to focus on each link separately, and I want to do that starting with the first link, even though we do not differ on that first link—we both believe in God because we think it is true—or the second link—we both are Christians because we believe in Christ's claim to be divine—or even *some* of the third link—you do call yourself a Catholic, although only a "cafeteria Catholic". But even though we agree about them, we need to explore the two prior links of the chain first in order to understand my reasons for being a non-cafeteria Catholic, or a "full-course-meal Catholic". For the same arguments that justify my theism and my Christianity also justify my non-cafeteria Catholicism.

I assume we agree about the very first principle: that the only honest reason anyone should believe in God is because it is *true* that God is real. In fact, the only reason any honest person ever ought to believe in anything at all is truth. Any other reason for believing in anything, if it is not subordinate to truth, is simply dishonest. That applies no matter how important your motive or reason for believing may be.

Take two very important other motives: happiness and morality. When you were three, you believed in Santa Claus, you thought he was real, you thought the idea was true. You were wrong, the idea was not true (literally, at least, which is how you took it). But you did get two other very important things out of that idea: it made you very happy, and it made you very good, or at least very well-behaved before Christmas. Perhaps it was a shallow and selfish and childish happiness and goodness, but being happy and being good are very important things, so anything that increases them is important. So why don't you believe in Santa Claus today? If you did, it would make you happier and perhaps also better.

Because it isn't true. Truth trumps everything. I assume we both agree about that.

So why do we think God is true and not a mere myth like Santa Claus? What was our first reason for believing in God when we were children? Surely it was our trust in the authority of our parents. They taught us about God. And we believed their authority. That's the main way all children in all cultures learn everything at first: by trusting the authority of their parents. Then we gradually expanded that authority to friends and other adults, teachers, and books, and we also started to do our own personal thinking in evaluating these authorities. We found some friends and some other adults and some teachers to be more reliable than others. We had reasons for preferring one authority to another. We started to think critically and rationally and personally.

And our experience of the real world brought into question some of our former beliefs. Perhaps our experience of apparently undeserved suffering and apparently unanswered prayer brought into question our belief in an all-powerful, all-knowing, and all-loving God. Some of us came to think that we had good enough reasons to keep believing in God, and some of us thought the opposite. Some of us thought that natural science's explanations were sufficient for everything and that we didn't need any supernatural explanations for anything, so we exchanged God for science. Others—

most of us, including you and me—found ways to keep our faith in God. We thought we had reasons that would explain suffering and evil without abandoning either God or science.

But why did we not *want* to abandon God? The logical reason (as distinct from psychological or emotional reasons) was because we thought we had good reasons to trust our parents and other religious authorities. We may have had only weak reasons for our faith in God, but we also had strong reasons for our faith in our parents and teachers, for trusting those authorities. Especially Jesus' authority. If God did not exist, then Jesus was the most seriously deluded man who ever lived.

We find the same pattern when it comes to believing in Christ. Our first reason for believing in Christ, like our first reason for believing in God, was the authority of our parents and teachers. Then we started to think for ourselves, and we found some good reasons to back up our faith. Christ claimed to be divine, and He seemed to be a trustable authority, the kind of person every trustable person trusted. If He was not God, then He must have been either a liar, if He knew He wasn't God, or a lunatic, if He thought He was God but really wasn't. Or else, if we did not think this way, if we did not find any such reasons, we eventually either abandoned our faith in Christ or, to keep our faith, we abandoned our demand to have good reasons for our faith. I think we both agree that both of those last two options are tragic, because both faith and reason are necessary and to throw away either one is a very great loss.

The same reasoning applies to the Church. Reason led us to God, God led us to Christ, and Christ led us to the Church that He established and to which he gave His authority. ("He who hears you, hears me", He said to His apostles.) Each step in the argument appeals to the previous one. And each step in the argument is an either/or. If God does not exist, then believers are as stupid as grownups who still believe in Santa Claus. If Christ is not the Lord, then He is the world's biggest liar or lunatic. And if the Church is not what she claims to be, then she is the most arrogant and wicked false prophet in the world. In each of the three cases, if you reduce the divine to the human, it becomes almost subhuman, the worst and lowest of human possibilities. If the Church is an arrogant, idolatrous, blaspheming, and sacrilegious false prophet, you do not want to step one foot into that cafeteria or eat one bite of its food.

Now here we are, two honest people who agree about the essence of the chain, which is truth. We are also two theists who agree about the first link, God. We are also two Christians, who agree about the second link, Christ. And we partly agree and partly disagree about the third link, the Church, since you do identify yourself as some kind of Catholic. But as a "cafeteria Catholic", you accept only parts of that link, while I accept all of it. You have two and a half links; I have three.

If you were an atheist, I would appeal to our common reason to try to lead you to God. If you were a Jew or a Muslim, I would appeal to our common agreement about God in your scriptures as well as mine; I would appeal to your authorities about God to try to lead you to Christ. So now as a Christian, I appeal to Christ as our common authority to lead you to believe the whole claim of the Catholic Church.

For just as God is one and Christ is one, so the Church is one. My argument against your "cafeteria Catholicism" is that just as God is all-or-nothing, and so is Christ, so is the Church. You cannot have half of God or half of Christ, and you also cannot have half of the Church. She claims to be "the Body of Christ". Either she is or she isn't. She can't be half a body. Half a body is a corpse. It's all or nothing, life or death.

Let's look at that parallel logically. God is either real or unreal. If God is unreal, then theists are simply wrong, completely wrong, not partly wrong, about whether God is real. And if Christ is not divine, then Christians are simply wrong, completely wrong, not partly wrong, about Christ, about whether Christ is divine. And if the Church is not what she claims to be, then Catholics are not just partly wrong but simply wrong, in fact, very, very wrong, about the Church. For if the Church is not the divine, infallible authority she claims to be, then she is the world's most insufferably arrogant and blasphemous false prophet saying "Thus saith the Lord" for merely fallible human opinions.

You cannot be half a theist, and you cannot be half a Christian, so you cannot be half a Catholic, either. Did you ever hear of a "cafeteria theist" or a "cafeteria Christian"? You cannot have half of God or half of Christ, and neither can you have half of the Church. If God is not God, religion is not half right, it is the worst error of all. If Christ is not God, He is not a good man but the world's worst liar or lunatic. And if the Catholic Church is not the one truest and best church, she is the falsest and worst, and the restaurant that serves your "cafeteria Catholicism" deserves to be shut down completely by the spiritual health authorities.

The argument is very simple and very strong, for all three links in the chain—God, Christ, and the Church—make claims that make neutrality or compromise logically impossible. The one and only thing all three cannot possibly be is something that is neither totally and absolutely good and right and true nor totally and absolutely evil and wrong and false, but something between the two, a cafeteria with everything in it up for grabs, at the choice of the consumer. If God does not exist, believers are not just mistaken but insane—as insane as adults who believe in the reality of their imaginary childhood heroes or in Santa Claus. If Christ is not God, He is not a nice man but the most insane lunatic or the most wicked liar who ever lived. And if the Church does not speak with His authority but only with her own, she is history's biggest liar and most arrogant false prophet, and "keep the faith" really means "keep the fake". It is logically everything or nothing all three times.

You can go up this ladder as well as down. Start with the Church. She claims divine authority. Apparently ridiculously arrogant. Why does she do that? Only one thing can possibly justify it. All other reasons leave her as the worst false prophet. It is Christ who justifies it, Christ's words, Christ's promise, Christ's institution, Christ's task to her to proclaim with His authority His gospel and dispense His salvation through His sacraments. And what justifies Christ in claiming divine authority? Only one thing: His Father has authorized Him, and He is totally obedient to His Father and has the same divine nature as His Father. Nothing else could justify it. If He is anything less than divine, He is something less than human.

Of course, there is a difference among these three links. God is simply God. Christ is not only God but also man, not only infinite and immortal but also finite and mortal. And the Church is not only infallible in her official "ex cathedra" dogmas and commandments but also fallible in all her human judgments. Christ is perfect not only in His divine nature but also in His human nature, but the Church's human nature, like ours, is far from perfect. She has a divine nature, too, for she is the Body of Christ, but she also has not only a human nature but a very imperfect human nature.

In that sense, I too am a "cafeteria Catholic". I do not agree with many of the things our bishops and our pope say when these merely human authorities seem to me not to line up with the infallible, authoritative teachings that are the Sacred Tradition that the Church has always taught with the authority of Christ and His apostles, or when their non-authoritative teachings and prudential decisions do not seem at all reasonable to me, like the Inquisition, the treatment of Galileo, or Pope Francis' trust in the atheistic Communist rulers of China to help choose bishops for the Catholic Church in China.

Here is another example of legitimate disagreement. I do not agree with the paragraph that the present pope personally inserted into the catechism about capital punishment. He said that capital punishment is not only no longer practically necessary to protect the innocent in an age of generally fair jury trials and secure prisons (I have no disagreement with that opinion) but is also in principle wrong in itself. I think the pope was simply wrong about that, because the Church has always taught the opposite: that the State does have the right to execute murderers and traitors and terrorists if necessary to protect the innocent, because the right of self-defense against unjust aggression is a right of States as well as individuals. The State may wisely choose not to exercise that right, but it has that right. Francis was also wrong to tell Catholics to stop "obsessing" over abortion. That is like telling German Jews to stop obsessing over Hitler's Holocaust.

By the way, did you notice your immediate knee-jerk reaction to my last sentence? You probably thought: How dare

I classify abortion as anything like the Holocaust? You do not allow anyone to compare any other evil to the Holocaust. You feel it is an insult to Jews, especially to survivors of the Holocaust. Well, if nothing else can be compared to the Holocaust, then the Holocaust cannot be compared with anything else, either, and in that case the Holocaust loses its moral relevance. If there are no smaller holocausts, then the great one loses its teaching authority. And then prophets like Elie Wiesel should stop saying "Never again!" Because it is happening again in many places, though not exactly in the same way. If other tyrants, like Stalin and Mao and Castro and Pol Pot, cannot be compared with Hitler, Hitler loses his relevance. If cruel and oppressive bosses that treat their employees like slaves cannot be compared to literal slave owners, if they are not at least a little bit like slave owners, then they cannot be said to have at least some of the evil that slave owners have. So if abortion is not wrong for the same reason the Holocaust was wrong, then you cannot condemn abortion at all because that is the only thing wrong with it: that it is murder. The objective evils are the same, even though the subjective motives are not. Both abortion and the Holocaust deliberately kill innocent human beings, even though the conscious motives of aborters are far less evil and hateful and less clear and conscious than the motives of the architects of the Holocaust. Whatever is *sui generis*, whatever is unique and not in the same moral genus (good or evil) as all other goods or evils, is no more relevant to those other goods or evils than color is to shape or shape to color.

I have a suggestion for how "liberals" can become pro-life instead of pro-choice. If you can label unborn babies as convicted murderers, you can apply your condemnation of capital punishment to abortion.

By the way, I have never understood political categories like "liberal" and "conservative". What is "liberal" about "liberating" the souls of unborn babies from their bodies by crushing their skulls, cutting off their limbs, or poison-burning their skins? Saying "I'm not pro-abortion, I'm just pro-choice" makes exactly as much sense as saying "I'm not pro-slavery, I'm just pro-choice." Saying "If you disapprove of abortion, don't have one, but don't impose your morality on me" makes exactly as much sense as saying "If you don't approve of having slaves, don't have one, but don't impose your morality on me." Which was exactly what Southern slave owners said to Northern abolitionists.

I also never understood why "conservatives" were not in the forefront to conserve the very planet they live on.

I'm wandering. Sorry. But it is worth saying, so I let it stand.

My point for our debate is that we Catholics are perfectly free to be "cafeteria Catholics" about things for which the Church does not claim divine authority. But whatever is part of her claim to infallibility is like Christ's claim to divinity: it is either sacred or sacrilege. It deserves either the bended knee or the swift kick. But not toleration. We do not "tolerate" true prophets of God; we believe them and obey them and canonize them as saints. We do not "tolerate" false prophets, either; we excommunicate them.

In other words, we non-cafeteria Catholics do exactly what you rightly demand we do: we do not leave our reason at the door of the church. We discriminate, we judge, we are "judgmental". We use both reason and faith; we appeal to both; we do not refuse the authority of either of those two inventions of God, though we do use them to question all other authorities, including political and social and cultural authorities, such as the ones to whom you appeal to justify your cafeteria Catholicism, namely, the popular consensus of a decadent and de-Christianized culture.

We non-cafeteria Catholics question all human authority, and we believe and obey divine authority, and we have good reasons for doing both and for distinguishing between the two. We do not put the tag "Thus saith the Lord" on the political party platform of either the donkey or the elephant. Nor do we reduce the Man who did put the tag "Thus saith the Lord" on His words to a super social worker or a pop psychologist preaching platitudes. Nor do we reduce the Catholic Church to one of 30,000 "denominations".

~

We both believe in God. But how do we know the true God? Through Christ. How do we know Christ? Through the Church.

You say you admire Catholic theology because it is not "fundamentalist" and because its God is bigger than Santa Claus for Adults or the Big Guy in the Sky. Good. But I hope you don't mean that you admire it, not because it is true, but because it is a great work of art. The objects of art are man-made. The objects of science are not. Theology is a science, not an art. This applies to both dogmatic theology and moral theology. It is a science. It is not creation, it is discovery. It is not an empirical or mathematical science, of course, so it does not use the scientific method, but it is a science. It is a knowing, not a feeling or a making or an invention or a kind of spiritual technology.

I think we both use the word "fundamentalist" to mean "literalist". You admire Catholic theology because it is not "fundamentalist", i.e., literalist. Of course you are right.

Images and symbols are not to be taken literally. (E.g., "God sits on His mighty throne. His right hand is full of power.") But much of theology is literal even though its images are not. Only negative theology (what God is not) is completely literal: God is literally not an animal, an abstract idea, or a stone idol. In contrast, affirmative language about God (what God is) is not literal but analogical: e.g., God's justice and knowledge and power are not the same as man's. His are not like ours, but ours are like His, as an image is like a person, but a person is not like an image. But even analogical theology is literal in another sense: it is not mere metaphor. It is a metaphor to say that God sits on a throne dispensing justice by his "strong right hand", or to call God a "rock" or a "lion". Literally speaking, that is not true. God is "above" us in perfection, but not above us in space. "Above" is a mere image or metaphor. God is more like a rock than like a cloud and more like a lion than like a mouse, but he is neither a chemical nor an animal. Those are mere metaphors. But God's power and justice and life are not metaphorical, though they are analogical. That is to say that they are not the same as ours, as a saint's goodness is not the same as a baby's goodness, but not wholly different, either. God's love is also analogical but not metaphorical. It is analogical because it is both essentially the same kind of thing as our love, namely, the will to the good of others, but it is also not the same as ours in at least two ways: it is not conditioned by passive emotional changes, and it is wise enough to allow us to suffer for our own good. Our love waxes and wanes with our feelings, and our wisdom is so limited that it is rare that we rightly make others suffer for their own good. I think you understand and believe this.

What troubles me most is that sentence of yours where you say you would accept God even if He turned out to be merely our personification of love. Let's examine that word. "Personification" means treating as a person something that is not really a person, like calling a pet or a car or a house by a human name. But God IS a person—three, in fact—and the one thing you cannot ever personify is a person!

"God is love" does not mean that God is an abstraction, that God is a "value". When you die, you will not meet an abstraction, and you will not be sent to Heaven by an abstraction. That would be like meeting a number or being sent to Bermuda by the Bermuda triangle.

A personification is the effect of the human act of personifying. An act of personifying is a human act, like a song. It depends on us. If God is a personification, then he is our product, our effect rather than our cause, and we are really worshipping ourselves. That is the ultimate idolatry. You should worship your Creator, not your creations. God must be something prior and greater than you, not the work of your own hands or the work of your own mind. Worshipping your own creations is like giving birth to your own mother.

I am going to assume that that sentence about personification that I quoted from your letter was a slip of the pen, that you do not really mean it. Because it is almost worse than atheism. If you really mean it, it means you do not even care whether God is real or not.

And not caring about whether God is real—the God who is love itself—means not caring about whether love "goes all the way up", so to speak, into the nature of absolute reality; not caring about whether love is the very essence of ultimate reality (=God) or only a subjective human desire or deed or choice or ideal or dream or value, something abstract. In that case, it is not something like a real house that we can live in or a real horse that we can ride on, but only something we can think about and admire, like a song.

I will give you the credit of not quite meaning what you say or saying what you mean there. I think you meant to say something like this: When I die, if I found out that the real God is not love at all but hate (a truly horrible thought-experiment!), then I would love and worship the abstract ideal of love rather than the concrete person of the God who is hate. If that is what you mean, I agree with you. We worship God, not because He is all-powerful, but because He is all-good, and love is the supreme good.

We need to think more about what we mean by "love".

3. Love

You say that "God is love." I agree. You say that love is the meaning of life, that love is life's greatest value. I agree. You say that everyone knows that, deep down, by conscience. I agree.

But I hope you do not mean, when you say that "God is love", that "love is God". Sentences are not equations. And when you say that love is the meaning of life, I hope you do not mean that love as a *feeling* is the meaning of life. Or that moral conscience, which commands love, is also a feeling. Because most people do mean those three mistakes today.

Mistake #1: "God is love" and "Love is God" mean very different things. Look at the structure of a sentence. The subject is like the title, and the predicate is like the book or the speech. The predicate tells you something new about a subject with which you are already familiar. So "God is love" means: "I'm going to tell you something new and startling and wonderful about the God you already know: His very essence is love." "Love is God" means: "I'm going to tell you something new and startling and wonderful about the love you already know, the finite, fallible, frequently foolish feeling you already know: that is God, that is the highest thing, look no further."

"God is love" is a sentence, not an equation. It is not reversible.

Mistake #2: God is love. But what is love?

Love, according to the Church, the Bible, Jesus, and the vast majority of all saints, sages, and philosophers before Rousseau, is not a feeling. It is *commanded* by Jesus, and Jesus is a good psychologist. He knows that feelings cannot be commanded. "I command you to have sweet, nice feelings toward everybody" is simply stupid, and Jesus is not stupid.

Love is accompanied by many feelings, and feelings can be very good and helpful, but love is not a feeling. Love is a free choice of the will. To love is to will the best good and the truest happiness of the other person.

This is not just Catholic dogma and divine revelation and an appeal to faith. Everyone knows it by experience. We all know the supreme test of true love for another person is self-sacrifice, the willingness to suffer for another. We may say we do not know this, or that we disagree with this, but our lives prove the opposite: that we do know it and recognize it when someone gives us this kind of love (e.g., sacrificing his life for us). We recognize it even when he sacrifices his time for us, for time is life: part of a "life-time".

Love as a feeling is more immediate fun, of course. As Dostoyevsky said, "love in action (*agape*) is a harsh and dreadful thing compared with love in dreams (the feeling)." But love in action is the love that has power to change lives. We know this if we have children. Life is a gift, and we give it to our children (and to all our descendants) only because we have been given this gift first by our parents. We give what we have been given. We cannot possibly give back to our parents a just and equal return for the gift of life that they give us. We cannot pay it back, so we "pay it forward". We pass on to our children the gift our parents gave us when they laid down their lives for us: we lay down our lives for our children. We give what we have been given. That is the strategy of God's great invention of the family. This is not the love that is a feeling (though it is powerfully motivated by feelings, and it also produces feelings of great happiness as well as great worries and frustrations), but it is the love that is a fact and a power: the fundamental fact and the fundamental power of human history.

Mistake #3: What is true of love is also true of conscience: conscience is also not a feeling. It is more simple and sober and unspectacular than feeling. It is a knowing, an immediate, intuitive knowing of good and evil. It is like recognizing a color. People who have suppressed their conscience (I do not say people without a conscience, because there is no such thing) are like people with color blindness, but in this case it is a blindness that is self-induced. Like love, conscience is *accompanied* by feelings—feelings of obligation before we do a deed and feelings of guilt or self-approval afterward. But it is not in its essence a feeling.

Feelings are often deceptive. Addicts have strong feelings of love and desire for their drugs. Hate is also a very strong and very deceptive feeling. We cannot live freely if we are chained to our feelings any more than if we are chained to our drugs. "It can't be wrong because it feels so right" is one of the stupidest song lines in history. Hitler could have sung that song. Feelings are like horses: powerful and beautiful but in need of riders (minds and wills) to direct them rightly rather than either suppressing them by tying them up in chains (Stoicism) or by blindly obeying them by letting them run wherever they will (Rousseau). That's just common sense, at least to every successful culture in history. It is almost the definition of civilization. It is the virtue of self-control, temperance, or moderation. Its opposite is addiction. And since addiction is the opposite of freedom, self-control is almost the definition of freedom. But self-control, especially sexual self-control, is the single most unpopular of all traditional Catholic (and pagan!) values today.

~

We agree that "God is love." But how do we know that? From the Bible? But it was the Church (the apostles) that wrote the Bible (the New Testament), and it was the Church that later defined it, canonized it. How do you know the four Gospels belong to it but the Gnostic gospels do not? How do you know the Epistle of James belongs in it? Luther called James "an epistle of straw". It is the Church that told us what books are in it, and it is the Church that declared it divine revelation.

I sympathize with your objection to the Church. As G. K. Chesterton said, there is only one really strong argument against Christianity: Christians. Fortunately, Christianity is not the worship of Christians, it is the worship of Christ.

Yes, it is true, as you say, that those who claim to be God's representatives are sometimes arrogant and angry and self-righteous, especially the fundamentalists. But Catholics are not fundamentalists. If American Catholics today have a typical fault, it is the opposite: they are more like Ned Flanders in "the Simpsons". They're not too hard, they're too soft. They're not hot spice, they're cold oatmeal. They reduce their religion to "Here comes everybody. Smile."

It is also true, as you say, that God is not arrogant or angry or hateful. "The wrath of God" is an anthropomorphism, just like "God sits on a high throne and has a strong right hand." It is symbolic language: thrones and strong right hands are symbols of rule. God is love, not hate, and because He loves us, He hates our enemies. His hate is directed against sins, not sinners, just as the hate of the loving surgeon is directed against the cancer, not against the patient. Good grief, Nat, didn't you learn that in catechism when you were about five years old? The more you love the sinner, the more you hate whatever is harming him, and sin harms not just his body but his soul. How much simpler could it be?

4. Freedom

You are also right about your other pop culture quotation, the movie title "Whose Life Is It, Anyway?" That is indeed the question. But you are wrong about the answer if you agree with the movie's pro-suicide philosophy. Your life is not your own, unless you are God or unless you created yourself. As God asked Job at the end of that book, "Were you there when I designed and created you? I didn't notice you sitting with the angels giving Me advice."

It is not your life, or mine; it is God's. We are to God what Hamlet is to Shakespeare. We did not invent Him; He invented us. We did not make Him in our own image; He made us in His image. We did not give Him life; He gave us life. If that is not true, then there is no God. Belief in a mere ideal or value, a God who is an abstraction, is a form of atheism. And so is a mere deistic disinterested observer God or a mere pantheistic impersonal force. I think you agree with that, but I think you also forget it.

Augustine distinguished two meanings of freedom. The lesser one, free will or free choice (*liberum arbitrium*), is a means to the greater one, *libertas*, liberty, freedom from all evil: both sin and suffering. We cannot ever be without the first kind of freedom, free will. Everyone has that. We have no free choice about whether or not we have free will. But we do have free choice about the second kind of freedom. We can use the first kind of freedom, free will, either to attain the second kind, liberty, or to give up the second, to sell ourselves freely into slavery. Everyone who becomes an addict does that. They use their freedom to give up their freedom. They forge the chains of their slavery with the power of their freedom.

And that is all of us. We are all sinaholics, sin addicts, self-ishness addicts. That is why we are very stupid if we try to "create our own values" because we want to be "free" from the moral law, which feels (to our foolish and selfish egos) like a suit of foreign, constricting armor. That is an example of the fallibility of feeling. The moral law, as distinct from man-made "positive laws", the "natural moral law" that is based on our human nature, is the blueprint for freedom, not constriction. Saints are free by their detachment from their own egos and disordered desires—free from addiction, which is slavery. You are a slave to whatever you cannot part with that is less than yourself.

In Hell, all are "free" to create their own values. And they do. That is what Hitler did. And the Devil, when he revolted. In Heaven, everyone is really free (without the snarky quotation marks) because they value what is truly valuable: God and all His works, including the real world and themselves as the unique part of that world that reflects His image, that can conform to His values and, in so doing, experience joy. For every living thing experiences joy when it is true to its own nature and experiences misery when it is not. That is part of what "natural law" means.

If you say to me: "Love me, love my freedom", you are right. Therefore, I will not compel you, but I will try to teach you. I will not be like the Godfather, who makes you an offer you can't refuse. I will be like God the Father, who makes you an offer you can refuse.

The Church is not God, but she is God's public prophet. As I admitted before, this prophet has a spotty track record in practice when it comes to respecting people's freedom. All too often those in authority tried to compel faith, whether by military force, political force, or even, in rare but real occasions, the force of torture. It was a really stupid mistake.

But please do not equate the Church's teaching with the Spanish Inquisition. Labeling some human acts good and helpful to the flourishing of human nature, and others as bad and harmful, is not torture or even force; it is just truth. Just because the x-ray tells you that you have a disease, and that makes you unhappy, that does not mean that the x-ray is not true or that the x-ray technician hates you. In fact, it means he loves you, because one of the most important things love does is that it refuses to lie; it tells the truth to all the persons who are loved, even if they don't like it and even if the teacher is hated in return for his love.

Take a typical instance. Nearly all people, including Protestant Christians, criticize the Church for being rigid, unbending, cruel, and impersonal for not allowing divorce. But the reason she says this is because Jesus said it, quite clearly, in the Gospels. Why did He say that? Because He is love incarnate, and He wants us to be deeply, truly happy, and divorce is one of the most profound causes of unhappiness in human life. The data—the scientific data—show very strongly and clearly that children are more traumatized by their parents' divorce than by a parent's death. The Church forbids divorce, not because she is less compassionate and kind than all other Christian denominations, which do. Exactly the opposite: because she is *more* kind and compassionate. And divorce not only harms children, it harms society in harming society's most important, most loving, and most happifying institution, marriage; in making marriage undoable, revocable, revisable, negotiable. It takes half the drama and romance out of it. It cuts asunder what God has put together. For marriage was God's invention, not man's. That is very clear in Genesis and in Jesus.

Jesus forbade divorce, and so does the Catholic Church, but other Christian churches try to correct their Lord's "cruel and uncompassionate" mistake on this score. Only the Catholic Church is humble enough not to claim that authority. The same goes for all other aspects of the sexual morality that was common to all Christians, and even many pagans, until the Sexual Revolution. You know what they are. They are by far the most common reason Catholics leave the Church today. For two thousand years, there has never been a single teaching of the Church's Magisterium (teaching authority) that has been so massively hated, rejected, and disobeyed as *Humanae Vitae*.

Catholics have very countercultural dogmas, thank God, but they do not have very countercultural practices, alas. Catholic practice is not much better than non-Catholic practice in all the areas of sexual morality: masturbation, pornography, fornication, contraception, abortion, adultery, sodomy, transgenderism. But we do not claim infallible divine authority for our practices, only for our dogmas. We are not saints; we are sinners. The Church is not a museum, but a hospital; not a throne room, but a bathroom. We stink. That is why we have the sacrament of confession. It's a spiritual toilet bowl.

There are only two kinds of people who do not think they need that sacrament: people who do not believe the x-ray and people who do not believe the surgeon; people who do not believe the bad news about sin and people who do not believe the good news about forgiveness and healing. In other words, the proud and the despairing. Two of the deadliest of deadly sins.

Why should that traditional morality apply to every part of human life *except* sex? Why should there be only one moral rule about sex, namely, "respect everyone's free consent"? The new morality says that everything sexual is OK as long as there is no force; that the only sexual sin is the sin against "freedom". Why don't we say that about anything else? Why don't we apply that to a bad war to which both sides, who hate each other, consent? To cannibalism? To suicide? To drugs? To sadomasochism? To education? "I freely choose to ruin my life, my mind, my freedom of will, my happiness, my human nature." "That's OK, as long as that's your choice."—Do we say that to anyone we love?

Why, then, do we make an exception in sex? Why do we require truth and justice and respect and unselfishness and self-sacrifice and non-betrayal everywhere else, but tolerate an "anything goes" in sex? Why do we defend impersonal, selfish, shallow, materialistic, meaningless sex, but not impersonal, selfish, shallow, materialistic, meaningless anything else?

Well, isn't it obvious? Because compared to other impersonal, selfish, shallow, materialistic, and meaningless enterprises, sex still *feels* pretty darn good.

You say: "Love me, love my freedom." I quite agree! Therefore, if I see you giving up your freedom and becoming an addict—whether to drugs, to alcohol, to pornography, to selfishness, to your smartphone, to sex, or to money —it is not because I don't care about your freedom but because I do. That is why I say "Stop!" Mothers who yell at their children, "Get off the thin ice!" are not destroying their children's freedom but preserving it.

The Church wants to mother you, not smother you; father you, not bother you; teach you, not leech you; save you, not enslave you. Some churchmen (and churchwomen) are power-greedy egotists, but the Church is more than the average sanctity level of her members. She is holy. She was instituted by God in the flesh. She is God's collective prophet to the world. She sees many things you do not see, such as the unimaginable joys of Heaven and the unimaginable misery and despair of Hell.

The Church's condemnation of radical feminism, pornography, sodomy, transgenderism, divorce, abortion, contraception, fornication, masturbation, and lust is not a condemnation of feminists, addicts, gays, lesbians, transgenders, divorcees, pro-choicers, contracepters, fornicators, masturbaters, and lusters. It is her attempt to free us from these spiritual diseases by telling us the truth. There is such a thing as human nature, and that is why there *is* a "one size fits all" morality: because all men are created equal. The iron armor that constrains and imprisons us and does not fit us is not holiness, sanctity, moral virtue, or chastity (which is simply moral virtue concerning sex) but sin, including sexual sin.

And the Church's condemnation of these things is so cowardly and wimpy that it is almost nonexistent. When is the last time you heard a homily about sexual morality?

And why were those the only sins you mentioned? Why is sex the only area of Catholic morality non-Catholics and "cafeteria Catholics" obsess about? It's not our obsession, it's yours.

You are right about Sinatra's song "I Did It My Way."

That is the song that "threatens" us Catholics the most—because that is Satan's song.

And the right answer, the lover's answer, to Paul Newman's question "Whose life is it, anyway?" is indeed, as you say, "yours". When we say "my whole life is yours" to another human being, that's called marriage. When we say it to God, it's called religion and faith and worship. Because if God created us, our life is His whether we admit it or not. If we created ourselves, then we are the answer to that question. But we did not (duh!). Our lives are a gift from Life Itself. That's why they are precious and why the Church has a lot of strict laws about life. You don't surround rocks or paper clips with fences and strict laws, only diamonds and palaces.

5. Natural Law

Your next paragraph begins with the excellent question: What is it to be a human being? And you begin by rejecting two opposite forms of predestination: from below (materialism) and from above (Calvinism). Good. But then you embrace a position that logically fits only with atheism: the idea that since it is not true that "biology is destiny", we are free and not destined at all, or that our only destiny is to be free. But there is not an either/or contradiction between freedom and destiny. If we are in a meaningful story, there must be both of these dimensions: freedom (in the characters) and destiny (from the author), somehow mysteriously intermingled. You think they exclude each other, and you affirm the freedom and eliminate the destiny or design, which is as bad as the opposite mistake that you rightly refute, affirming the destiny and eliminating the freedom.

You say the only nature you have is determined by our freedom. But that is simply not true. Our freedom did not create our nature; God did.

We also do not have the freedom to change our essential nature. We cannot become an angel, a mere animal, an extraterrestrial, or an elf. It is our nature that determines (i.e., that structures and defines) our freedom, not vice versa. We are like travelers on a road that forks: we make the travel but not the road. At every moral fork in the road, we have the freedom to choose between good and evil, but we do not have the freedom to make good into evil or evil into good, any more than we have the freedom to make eastbound roads take us west or westbound roads take us east.

In fact, unless there is a "natural moral law", a system of objective moral values that defines and determines some things, like murder and rape, as evil and other things, like justice and charity, as good, our choices can have no real moral meaning. We cannot and do not invent the fundamental rules of human life. We discover them. That is what conscience is. It is not creative; it is not original; it is not like fiction. Saints never "create their own values". Who does? Sociopaths.

It is true, as you say, in fact, quite profoundly true, that we choose our own "who", our own individual personalities, by our choices; that God gives us only the raw material, the "what", and out of it we freely create the work of art that is our "who", our individual personalities and our lives. Living is indeed an art. But all art has some basic rules, and they are not arbitrary and not changeable. You are right to exalt freedom, but your kind of freedom undermines its own value by negating destiny and nature and natural law and objectively real meaning. Only in a world in which we are *not* free to say that saints are villains and tyrants are heroes can our freedom to choose between heroism and villainy be meaningful. I think you know enough about stories to see that.

(Please do not be insulted by the next few very elementary paragraphs about natural law. I do not know who understands this and who does not any more, because it is rarely taught, and even some very educated and very intelligent people do not understand its basic meaning.)

"Natural law" (i.e., the natural moral law) does not mean the laws of the physical world, which simply tell us how things do in fact behave. It means the laws of the moral world, which tell us how we ought to behave. It is called "natural" for two reasons: first, because it is based on human nature (e.g., moral laws about sex, speech, and property are based on the existence and nature of sex, speech, and property), and second, because we all know it by nature, as we know the laws of logic and mathematics by nature. The fact that our parents, teachers, and society teach us these laws does not mean that they invented them, as they invented "drive on the right" or "nine innings make a baseball game". Our parents and teachers teach us the laws of logic and mathematics, too, but they did not invent them. They invented only the languages by which we express them. The principles are not socially relative. There is no such thing as "Chinese logic" or "Japanese mathematics". And as far as the basic principles of the natural moral law are concerned, there is also no such thing as Chinese or Japanese morality. There are different social customs, because society creates those, but not different basic principles of morality for human nature, because society does not create human nature. God does.

That does not mean there are no moral differences between societies. There are, just as there are moral differences between individuals: differences in expression, in emphasis, and in degree of awareness and sensitivity, but not in basic principles. Some societies may even be blind to some basic principles (e.g., gypsies to the right to private property, Nazis or slavers to racial equality, and modern secularists and hedonists to the holiness of sex). But the existence of some color-blind people does not prove the subjectivity of color.

The Church defends the natural law by reason, not just by faith. She does not believe that an act is right or wrong simply because God wills it to be done or avoided. She adds many laws that are binding on Catholics only, but those are not the laws of nature but the laws of the house, so to speak. And she does not "impose" even the principles of the universal moral law on anyone, because they are there already. Einstein did not create and then impose the principles of relativity; he discovered them. Aristotle did not create and then impose the principles of logic; he discovered them. Euclid did not invent and then impose the principles of geometry; he discovered them.

Some laws are man-made and changeable. That is true of both secular laws (drive on the right) and ecclesiastical laws (fast on Good Friday, popes are elected by cardinals). But the fundamental laws of physics and mathematics are not man-made or changeable. Neither are the laws of biology. Neither are the fundamental laws of morality. They are based on our essential human nature, which is universal. Because we are rational beings, there are rational laws, laws about how to use our reason (e.g., honesty and truth-telling). Because we are emotional beings, there are laws about emotions (e.g., compassion vs. cruelty, and self-control vs. addiction). And because we are sexual beings, there are natural moral laws about sex. Rape, for instance, is not only wrong because it is assault but because it is sexual assault. It is not of the same moral quality as non-sexual assault; it is worse. A woman is to be treated somewhat differently from a man because a woman is somewhat different from a man. The oughts are based on what is. Moral values are based on facts.

I hope you do not disagree with that fundamental point,

that there is a natural moral law, a single moral law for the human nature that is common to all individuals and all societies at all times.

There are many differences between cultures about moral values, but these are all differences in *applications* of moral principles, all of which presuppose agreement about the basic principles. For instance, there are differences about when it is morally right to use lethal force (not all killing is murder), to deceive (not all deceptions are lies), or to remove someone's possessions by force (taking a madman's weapons is not stealing). But clearly a thing is not right just because you want to do it. The rules about how men and women should be treated differently and how they should be treated the same are partly the same (and universal) and partly different (and peculiar to different societies). The reason is clear: among individuals and among societies, some things are essential, universal, and unchangeable, and other things are accidental, particular, and changeable. That is clear and obvious. What is not so clear or obvious is just where that dividing line is. We can err by absolutizing what is only relative (our ancestors often tended to do that) or by relativizing what is absolute (that is what we tend to do).

If these universally known moral principles are violated, whether by individuals or by societies, we all instinctively and rightly judge those individuals or societies as morally *wrong*, not just by the standards of our society or of other societies, but by the standard of what everyone knows about human nature and its rights, by universal human conscience. If that is not so, then it was a hypocritical farce for the Nuremberg trials to condemn and punish the Nazi authorities. They were condemned, not for crimes against German or American or Russian law, but for "crimes against humanity".

There has never been a society that preached and practiced what Nietzsche called for, "a transvaluation of all values", a society that declared arbitrariness, oppression of the weak by the strong, arrogant pride, dishonesty, disloyalty, and the worship of power to be good, and declared reason, justice, humility, honesty, loyalty, and self-control to be evil. Every religion and every society in the history of the world has believed in that universal natural moral law that is founded on human nature. Our society, or at least the most influential mind-molders in our society, especially in media and higher education, is the first in history to deny it, and often to deny the very notion of "human nature", or essential natures of anything at all. But in the three thousand miles between Hollywood and Harvard are the vast majority of ordinary citizens who still believe and try to live by the natural law as known by conscience and as taught by every religion in the world.

You probably disagree with the Church's claim that the natural law includes the traditional principles of sexual morality, but I don't think you disagree with the rest of the natural law. You respond with moral indignation and protest when other people treat you with lies, injustice, cruelty, hate, harm, or betrayal. You appeal to their knowledge, by conscience, that these things are wrong. They know better, and that is why they ought to do better. I think you do in practice still believe in the old natural law. And you do not see that as contradicting our freedom—until it comes to sex.

That is how the Church is countercultural today. But the Church has always upheld the natural moral law even when parts of it were countercultural-—e.g., equality and compassion in a master/slave society like ancient Rome, care for the poor in societies that scorned them, and strict rules of warfare in violent societies. In the past, she has upheld the soft virtues (love, compassion, forgiveness, mercy, tolerance, sympathy) in hard societies, and today she is upholding the hard virtues (chastity, honor, honesty, justice, promise-keeping) in our soft society. She does not change, because the natural law does not change. We do. We sway and fall like drunks, first to the right, then to the left. She does not. Not even when many of her members do.

I am being "judgmental" here, as you imply, but not of your moral character or of your actions, which I do not know, but of your beliefs, which you have made known. And you are doing the same to me. One of us is right, and the other is wrong about whether moral law preserves or threatens freedom. We are not arguing about people (at least I am not) but about principles. Of course, if you no longer believe in any objective moral principles (any natural moral law), then judging people, and thus being "judgmental", is one of your only two remaining options. The other is ceasing to judge at all.

6. Conscience

If there is no natural law, no objective moral truth, then conscience can only be a subjective feeling. It cannot be an insight into objective moral truth if such truth does not exist.

I think you make three mistakes about conscience. Two of them are explicit, and one is implicit. I take the implicit one first because it is, I think, the foundation and premise for the other two and because it is the most common mistake people make today about conscience: that it is a feeling rather than a knowing and, therefore, subjective rather than objective.

Feelings are subjective, knowing is objective. What we feel is simply what we feel inside ourselves, but what we know is something outside ourselves, something that is real independent of our knowing, something that is there before we know it. But our feelings are not there before we feel them.

If conscience is simply a feeling about good and evil, if it is only subjective and individual, then we should not be "judgmental" about it. I should not be judged as wicked just because I feel crummy or as saintly just because I feel happy.

Knowing is also "subjective" in the sense that a concrete individual subject, or human person, is always its agent, its subject. But the *object* of knowing is not subjective.

So if conscience is a knowing, as is implied in the very word (*scio* means "I know"), then it is both objective (in its object) and subjective (in its subject). It is always I, or you, that knows. That is why one must never violate one's own conscience, one's own power to know the truth about moral good and evil: it is a sin against yourself, against your mind. It is a kind of dishonesty. Even if your conscience is wrong, you must obey it, since you do not know it is wrong. If my conscience tells me that it is wicked to bathe every day, I must not bathe every day. If it tells me it is wicked *not* to bathe every day, I must do it. Even an erring conscience binds, because you do not know that it is erring. You believe it is right, and you must live according to what you believe is true.

But conscience does not create truth; it discovers it (or tries to). It does not invent moral truth, as an artist invents art. We do not create values; we discover them, as we discover truths about past events (history) or matter (physics) or number (math) or how minds work (psychology). And we make many mistakes in that discovery process. We are mistaken if we think that the earth is the center of the universe or that any number of even integers can make an odd one or that there is no subconscious mind influencing the conscious mind. And we are equally wrong if we think that the Golden Rule of justice or the value of unselfish love or the dignity and intrinsic value of every person may be ignored—although *how* we know we are wrong is different in the different sciences. Ethics is a science, a knowing, though not the same kind as history, physics, math, or psychology.

Conscience is (1) our understanding of the meaning of moral concepts like "ought" and "ought not", "right" and "wrong", "good" and "evil"; (2) our knowledge of moral principles like "murder is wrong"; (3) our ability to apply these principles to situations like self-defense, capital punishment, war, or abortion (this is what we usually argue about, since situations, unlike principles, are complex and changing); and (4) our feelings of obligation or oughtness or duty to do (or avoid) an act before we do (or avoid) it and feelings of guilt or innocence after we do (or avoid) it.

Most people today reduce conscience to a feeling (element #4). But this feeling is not like feeling happy or curious or worried. It is a uniquely human feeling; animals do not have it. Animals may feel shame, but not guilt. Shame is only social, not individual. You feel ashamed to be naked in front of other people but not when you are alone. But you feel guilty even when you are alone.

Guilt is a feeling *about* something, thus it has content that is cognitive ("rational", in the old, broader sense). It is "intentional", like a sign. It signifies, it intends, it means, it points to something real. Like any sign, it may err. But the concept of error presupposes the concept of truth. If there is no objective truth, there can be no errors.

Your second error is to think that the Church "imposes" her morality on her people. It is not "her" morality. She did not invent it, she simply reminds us of it. The rules she makes for Catholics (go to Mass every Sunday) are not for non-Catholics, but the natural law is for everybody, and when society denies one part of the natural law, the Church upholds it. She is not afraid to be countercultural. That is not "imposition"; it is reminding.

In fact, the moral law *cannot* be "imposed" by force. Physical force overcomes freedom, but moral force, moral obligation, appeals to freedom. If I put a gun in your hand, force you to point it at someone, and force your finger to squeeze the trigger, I "impose" death by force, but I do not "impose" immorality on you; I do not make you a murderer, because your will is free and resists me, even when your body cannot. I cannot force you to be good or evil or to believe that any given act is good or evil. Truth cannot be "imposed". The truths of morality cannot be "imposed", any more than the truths of mathematics or physics can be "imposed".

You deny a "one size fits all" morality. But if we do not have a "one size fits all morality", then we do not have equal justice or equal rights; we have something like Nietzsche's "master morality" (might makes right for the "overman") against "slave morality" (equality and justice for the human sheep). One size does fit all, because we are all human.

We all have sexuality, and therefore sexual morality is also a "one size fits all" thing in its essentials, even though we have different subjective attitudes, beliefs, and feelings about it. Some of these differences are moral mistakes. E.g., some of us overdo the difference between men and women (e.g., a double standard, looseness for men [the "old boy network"] and tightness for women), and some of us underdo it (unisexism, transgenderism). The natural law is the only thing that justifies the judgment that both are mistakes even if society approves them. If there is no natural law that transcends the man-made laws of societies, then no society can be either better or worse than another. In that case, the millions of lives that we sacrificed to defeat Nazism were in vain. We were only fighting against military weakness, not against moral evil.

Today's holocaust is not racial but sexual. No nation ever lost one-third of its population to any war, but America loses one-third of its children to abortion. Abortion is an issue of sexual morality because it is murder justified by sex. Abortion is backup contraception, which is the demand to have sex without babies. So the Church has to be countercultural and unpopular today, just as she was in protesting the slave trade, which she did also in the name of the natural law. She has to be countercultural about contraception, too, because sex without babies is as unnatural as babies without sex (e.g., cloning). There was universal consensus against contraception in Christendom for 1900 years, until the Lambeth Conference in 1930. There was also universal consensus about sodomy, outside the Church as well as inside, until today. What next? Tomorrow, bestiality, incest, and group marriage may be seen to be as natural and innocent as contraception, sodomy, and now transgenderism are seen today. It takes only a single generation of media propaganda to reshape our minds like Play-doh. Once the natural law goes, *anything* can go. *Why not*, if it makes you happy for a moment, as long as it is free and consensual? Why not cannibalism? Why not "sexual suicide"? (Some find sexual excitement in killing themselves.) Whose life is it, anyway?

Your third mistake is a philosophical one: values are not the opposite of facts, unless you arbitrarily confine "facts" to empirical or mathematical propositions. Values are not the opposite of facts; values are facts of a certain kind. There are many kinds of facts besides "the sky is blue today" and "2+2=4". "There is (or is not) a Creator-God and a life after death", "Justice is a virtue", "Mother Teresa was a morally better person than Adolf Hitler", and "I feel happy today" are also facts. A fact is simply a true proposition. Different facts are known in different ways, but they are all true. Of course, there are many facts we do not know, and many things we think are facts that aren't, like "fake news".

Good moral arguments deduce values, not from facts alone, but from a value premise (some principle of the natural law, like "It is wrong to kill innocent human beings") plus a fact premise (like "unborn human babies are innocent human beings"). "Is" alone does not entail "ought", but every "ought" depends on some "is".

Natural law is not legalism. Legalism says that the only thing that counts morally is obeying the law. Natural law says that there are three things that count morally: the objective moral law, the subjective, personal motive, and the situation or circumstances. You have to do the right thing for the right reason and in the right way. Reducing morality to the first of those three things is legalism; reducing it to the second is subjectivism (because motives are subjective), and reducing it to the third thing is relativism (because situations are relative and changing). You make the same kind of simplistic, reductionist mistake as the legalist: legalists ignore factors 2 and 3; you ignore factor 1. A complete morality ignores none of them.

7. Sex

We now come to what for you is the heart of why you can call yourself only a cafeteria Catholic. If the Church only abrogated all her teachings about sex, I think you and millions of other American Catholics would have no more disagreements with her. All the heresies of the past are pretty much dead. You do not dispute the nature of Christ, the Trinity, the sacraments, or the relation between faith and works. You dispute sexual morality. That is your unique and historically unprecedented obsession.

That does not prove you are wrong, of course. It may be that all the religions in the world and all the cultures in the world and all the societies in the world at all times and places were wrong and you uprooted, ahistorical rebels in the peculiar culture that used to be called Christendom and is now largely ex-Christiandom or apostate Christendom—that you new kids on the block are right. But in light of the historical facts about how exceptional you are, do you have a right to be so unquestioningly certain that you are right and that the Church, which you admire in so many other respects, is wrong? (I say "unquestioningly" because you do not seem to be very skeptical of your skepticism.)

Is it not at least likely that your uniquely modern scorn and ignorance of history, your chronological snobbery, your disrespect for ancestry, might be blinding you to what everyone else used to see and still sees in other places (in Africa, for instance)? That the instinctive propriety and respect and honor and piety and holiness felt by the rest of the world and by the past toward sex is an insight rather than a superstition? Should you not at least keep your mind open when considering what the Church and all the other cultures before your own are claiming about sex, namely that it is holy, because it is not "the entertainment system" but "the reproductive system"? Even science calls it that.

Here is a good reason from experience for the Yes answer to the above questions: Your fundamental criticism is simply not true: belief in and obedience to the Church's teachings about sex do not remove or depress the importance and value and freedom and even the happiness of sex but, in fact, vastly increase all four of these things! Your own ancestors, before the Sexual Revolution, were by and large much happier in their sex lives than you and your generation are. There was no "sexual revolution" until the Sixties, not because the revolution was put down, but because it never rose up.

The main reason for this, the obvious reason, is the most fundamental sexual law of all, the law against adultery, i.e., the law that says that the place for sexual intercourse is inside marriage, not outside it. Of course that law was disobeyed spectacularly often by every culture in history, but the law was still there, and obedience was the norm, the default position, the base line, the assumption. It was assumed in the very breaking of it. The personal security that that law, like other moral laws, gives us is like the security that the fence around a baseball field surrounded by city streets gives to children who are playing on that field. It keeps them from running into the street and getting killed by cars. They are happier and freer with the fence than without it. They are not "free" to get killed. Death does not "free" us—unless you are a Gnostic and hate the body.

I don't think we moderns are too sexy, I think we are not sexy enough. Good sex, natural sex, real sex, is dying in our world. The very thrill of it is dying. Our world is like a theme park: an artificial, man-made, controlled imitation of the real, natural, dangerous, and thrilling thing; a safe and controlled Mount Everest or Harry Potter Hogwarts or Indiana Jones Temple of Doom. After a few rides, boring! Why is the real thing more interesting? Because God designed the real thing, and our redesigns of any thing can never top His in freedom, fun, felicity, and fascination. That is why we are more easily bored with the things we invent than with what God invents, namely, nature, the universe. Sex is fascinating because it is *not* "safe", either physically or emotionally or spiritually. Until it is tamed by the Revolution.

I am far from romanticizing the past. There was a lot of fear, ignorance, oppression, guilt, and perversion in the past about sex as there was about nearly everything else. Sin always spoils everything, in every age. But the amount of all five of these things in the present is even greater than it ever was in the past:

1. The fear of pregnancy is not a thing of the past but a thing of the present. The Pill did not remove that fear; it exacerbated it.

2. The primary result of modern sex education is ignorance of the most basic fact about sex: that its essential nature is for procreation, that sex is about children. Children are not its "accidents".

3. *You* feel oppressed today; your ancestors did not. Are you so arrogant as to say they were all ignorant of the fact

that they really were oppressed and unhappy even though they did not feel that way nearly as often as you do? Do you insist on "raising their consciousness" to where yours is, even though yours is not as happy and satisfied as theirs? Who is the judgmental oppressor here?

4. You have conquered guilt—except guilt about guilt. But guilt is good. Guilt is like pain: a sign that something is wrong. Ignore the signs at your peril. Eliminate all pain, and you will soon die. Eliminate guilt, and your soul will die.

5. Of course, there were sexual perversions and perverts in the past, but not as many as in the present. And they were not accepted, justified, sanctified, and glorified. At least perverts knew they were perverts. Today they parade their perversions. There are perversion *pride* parades! Perversions of all possible kinds, both heterosexual and homosexual, are celebrated. But perversions never work in the end. You cannot fool Mother Nature. Because Mother Nature is married to Father God, and modernity is an orphan because to it both its parents are dead.

I dare you to investigate Saint Pope John Paul II's "Theology of the Body". See if it isn't a bigger, happier, more human, and more profound philosophy of the meaning of sex than anything you ever dreamed of.

You complain that the Church's sexual morality is a "one size fits all" suit that ignores diversity. Why don't you say that about the rest of the Church's morality, e.g., the Golden Rule, the Ten Commandments, the Beatitudes, the four Cardinal Virtues, the three Theological Virtues, the three things that make any act good or bad (the act itself, the motive, and the circumstances or situation), the distinction between unchangeable principles and changing applications, the Church's economic morality (which is neither socialism nor unregulated laissez faire capitalism), her political morality (which does not coincide completely with either of our two parties' platforms), or her "just war theory", which repudiates both aggression and pacifism? Why are *they* not "oppressive" and "judgmental" and "one size fits all" suits for all to wear?

You prefer "diversity" to a "one size fits all" morality. But diversity from the natural moral law of rightness is by definition wrong, not right. There is in fact an amazing diversity in sexual opinions and sexual preferences and sexual desires and sexual activities. So what? Nothing about what ought to be logically follows from that. There is an amazing diversity in the ways we treat each other, in habits of treating each other, in all areas of life, not only sex; but not all of them are morally good. Some are virtues (good habits), and some are vices (bad habits). Why should diversity in opinions and practices in sex mean that all of them are good and none of them are bad, when diversity in any other area of human life does not mean that at all? Shouldn't we teach the same "one size fits all" universal virtues (honesty, justice, promise-keeping, trustability, responsibility, charity, goodwill, friendship, respect, unselfishness, self-control, wisdom, courage) in sexual behavior as everywhere else?

But of course we don't. Suppose there was some other act that had the same three consequences as divorce, but it had nothing to do with sex. We would never tolerate it.

What three consequences am I talking about? First, the abundant empirical evidence that divorce deeply and lastingly harms children—those innocent, vulnerable victims for whom parents are responsible.

Second, it also means welshing on the most solemn promise you ever make to the person you declared at the time to be the most important person in your life, your promise of lifelong love. (Remember, love as a feeling cannot be promised or commanded; only love as an act, a choice of the will, can be promised.) Why should anyone else ever trust you to keep any other, lesser promises when the #1 person in your life cannot trust you to keep the #1 promise in your life?

Third, it means the death of your society, for no society ever has survived or ever can survive without its fundamental foundation, namely, families that are stable and loving and therefore happy.

But, of course, divorce is fine because it's about sex: it gives you more sexual freedom.

Take abortion. Abortion is about sex because it is backup birth control, and birth control is the demand for sex without babies. It's the flip side of cloning or test-tube babies, which means babies without sex. If babies had nothing to do with sex, if the stork brought them, Planned Parenthood would go broke.

Why don't we think clearly about abortion? What, exactly and essentially, is abortion? Abortion means ending a pregnancy. How? There are only two ways: by giving the baby life or by giving the baby death; by having the baby or by killing the baby. Killing a baby is murder, because babies are innocent—they cannot commit any crimes—and they are human babies, not ape babies, at all stages of development. They do not become human at three or six or nine months or when the two blades of the scissors meet to cut the umbilical cord or when they first say "mama" or when they get a college degree and a good job. No other murder (deliberate killing of an innocent human being) is tolerated, but abortion is. Why? Because it is about sex. Doesn't that smell just a little suspicious?

The Church is only saying what all the authorities said until the Sexual Revolution. The modern position would have been perceived as just as outrageously out in left field in any pre-modern society as the Church's position is perceived to be in modern society.

And that includes what she says about contraception as an unnatural perversion. Almost nobody disagreed with that until the twentieth century, and now nearly everybody does. There are 30,000 Protestant denominations. Not a one of them allowed contraception until 1930. The very first one was, naturally, the Church of Henry's Hormones—oops, I'm sorry, the Church of England. (One of the many reasons I love Anglicans is that they can take all sorts of jokes at their expense.)

What about homosexuality? There is no other question today on which it is more fatal to speak the truth, so I anticipate that a lot of readers who made it this far with open minds will literally tear the next page or two out of this book and throw them into the fire and wish they could do the same to their author.

I love and respect many homosexual people. A few are good close friends. I also love many heterosexual sinners, starting with myself. But I do not love sins, any sins, including sexual sins, whether homosexual or heterosexual. And God Himself has declared, in His Book and in His Church, that homosexual acts are sins. (Not desires; desires are not under our free control. We are all born with disordered desires in many fields, including sex. It's activities that are morally good or bad, whether enacted or commanded or forbidden or permitted, by a free choice of the will.)

In the past, even those individuals and societies who justified homosexual activity (sodomy), like the upper classes in some of the ancient Greek city-states, tittered about it. It was never treated as a neutral thing that could equally "go either way". They knew it looked and felt unnatural.

Of course it is unnatural! Male and female sexual organs, like male and female human beings, are designed for each other, as obviously as nuts and bolts, or "male" and "female" electrical plugs. The whole world knew that.

By the way, the arguments for and against sodomy and contraception are identical. All arguments that justify or condemn either one do the same to the other.

Wait. Before you leave in disgust, remember that the Church has always said, and will always say, in an absolutistic and uncompromising and unalterable way, *two* things here, not just one: hate all sins and love all sinners. Homosexuals and heterosexuals are both sinners, and we are commanded to love both kinds of people, but neither kind of sins.

Those who want a changeable, negotiable, subjective sexual morality, which is now in fashion, risk a future change of fashion in which a newly fashionable hatred and persecution of homosexuals reappears, as it did in Nazi Germany; and if that happens, the Church will be the only institution that has any absolute and unchangeable moral principles left on which to rely in opposing that persecution and defending the intrinsic dignity of every person, including homosexual persons.

The Spanish Inquisition made the really stupid mistake of identifying heresies with heretics and thinking that it could wipe out sins and heresies by wiping out sinners and heretics. The moral relativists who run our society are making the exact same mistake of confusion and identification in reverse: loving heretics and therefore loving heresies, loving sinners and therefore loving sins.

And what group most adamantly protests against that distinction between sinners and sins, against the Church's principle to love the sinner and hate the sin? Homosexual activists, who always say that if you hate what they do, then you hate them, because they *are* what they do, that that is their essential identity. That is the very same mistake as was made by the Spanish Inquisition, and some day it may flip again upside down; and if it does, the Catholic Church will be the only refuge for poor, persecuted homosexual persons.

If the Church teaches all this, why don't you hear it from the pulpit? Two reasons: (1) Because it's illegal, it's "hate speech" in northern Europe and Canada, and if it becomes illegal here, the Church could be penalized, fined, and shut down for it. At the very least, she will be fiercely hated and mercilessly maligned by all the media mouths. And (2) because most Catholics, especially priests and bishops, are cowards. Like me. We long to be liked and hate to be hated. I have written almost one hundred books on almost every aspect of Catholic philosophy and theology, and this is the first time I have dared to open my big mouth more than an inch to defend the Church's two-thousand-year-old tradition on this hottest of hot button issues. (Actually it's more like a four-thousand-year-old tradition, because she inherited it from religious Judaism.)

Which brings us naturally (if I may use that maligned word) to the next issue, the horrible scandals of Catholic priests buggering little boys.

8. The Priest Scandals

Of course there is at least as much sexual abuse in all the other churches and in the public schools and in the entertainment industry and in sports as there is in the Catholic Church. But we are supposed to be living and defending a higher standard. What a really stupid and indefensibly weak excuse for sin it is to say "Everybody's doing it"!

It is equally stupid and indefensible to say that homosexuality is to blame for the priest scandals. It's priests who are to blame! Concrete persons, not abstract "orientations". Sins only come from sinners, and really wicked, really harmful sins come from really wicked sinners.

But most of those really wicked priests are homosexuals. That is simply a fact. Most homosexuals are not priests by any means, and most homosexuals are not pedophiles, but most pedophile priests are homosexuals. These are just statistical facts.

According to the most reliable statistics, about 5 percent of Americans are homosexual or bisexual rather than heterosexual. But over 80 percent of all cases of priests sexually abusing people—both pre-pubescent children and teenagers and adults—are homosexual. And the percentage of priests and bishops who are homosexual (in their primary sexual desire or orientation, if not in activity) is far greater than 5 percent. Everyone on the inside knows that there is indeed a very powerful "lavender Mafia" in the Church that goes all the way up into the most powerful Vatican offices. That is the gorilla in the room that no one mentions. Catholics are as cowardly as others in fearing the thought-police of political correctness.

One response to the scandal is to make a sharp distinction between pedophilia and homosexual intercourse with boys or men who are over the legal age limit of consent. Legally, this is an important distinction, but not morally. Which distinction is more important for morality, the State's or nature's? The State's legal age limit for consent to sex could be set at any age, like the draft age or the voting age or the drinking age; but the State does not define right and wrong, just legality and illegality. If sodomy is wrong, it is wrong with anybody, and it is more wrong with children not for any additional *sexual* reason, but for the additional reason that children are far more vulnerable and helpless and not able to give free consent.

Free consent is the only thing that counts in most of our secular culture today. In Germany, a cannibal advertised on the Internet for willing victims who consented to be eaten; he got twenty-eight. As long as it is free consent, it should be legal, say those thoroughly modern minds. Sadomasochistic orgies exist, by free invitation. They are not illegal in most states. The direct, deliberate killing of anyone who wants help in committing suicide is now legal in many American states and European countries. After all, reasons the typically modern mind, "whose life is it, anyway?" If there is no God and no natural law, free consent is the only thing that matters morally.

Most of the non-Christian population of the Western world now believes this unprecedentedly new philosophy. What does that have to do with priestly sex scandals? Well, some of these so-called "libertarians" would like to solve the problem by re-labeling it, not preventing it. They want the Church to agree with them and allow everyone, including priests, to have any kind of sex with any consenting adult at any time. That is what we have in *Brave New World*. That world is rapidly jumping out of its book and into our lives.

The Church is corrupt because the culture is corrupt and the Church is not countercultural enough. Do you want her to be *less* countercultural?

If anybody wants to leave the Catholic Church because of the priest scandals, he is of course free to go. Catholics are not a sect, like Scientology, that stalks and harasses its ex-members. But you will not find any safer place today than the Catholic Church, except the grave.

Certainly the safest place is not in a mother's womb. What other place has a 33 percent fatality rate?

If anybody was thinking of entering the Church and is deterred by the priest scandals, he was probably wrongly motivated to start with. The Church is not a museum for saints but a hospital for sinners. Her claim to be holy does not mean she claims to be sinless. It means she has the means for holiness, the "means of grace". She is the ark of salvation. God designed her, but the sailors who man her are often mediocre and uninspiring, and the animals on board are messing up the poop deck.

The Church is not a spiffy cruise ship. She is a big life raft. I laugh at people who malign "organized religion". I've never seen it. All I've seen is disorganized religion. Because all the people who do the work are amateurs.

Frankly, the Catholic Church's bureaucracy is unwieldy and all-too-human. Only a God with infinite patience and humor and love toward his severely brain-damaged children could possibly put up with it. (There are also many very good and holy and honest priests and parishioners—in fact they are the vast majority.)

It is not a business, it is a very large and dysfunctional family. Worst of all, it is a family that often thinks it is a business. But no merely human business that corrupt could possibly have lasted two thousand years. When Napoleon kidnapped the pope he said, "We will destroy your Church", and the pope laughed and said, "If we Catholics couldn't destroy her for 1800 years, you certainly won't."

Nor could any teaching institution survive that had as great a gap between the principles and the practice. What she teaches is perfect, divine love, the love whose name is Jesus Christ. What she practices is largely something else. There are only two ways to reduce that gap, Jesus' way and Machiavelli's way. Jesus' way is to bring the practice up to the level of the preaching. Machiavelli's way is to lower the preaching to the level of the practice. Jesus' way is very hard and Machiavelli's way is very easy, but do you really want her to exchange Jesus' way for Machiavelli's way?

9. Contraception

You say the Church's stance is "beyond the pale of argument" and comes from an "obsession" with sex. But in labeling sex a holy mystery, children its natural end, and contraception unnatural, the Church is simply repeating (a) a consistent part of the whole "Deposit of Faith" that she has received from Christ and the apostles and has been teaching for two thousand years (four thousand years, if you count her Jewish, pre-Christian form), (b) what all Christian authorities without exception, Protestant as well as Catholic, Anglican, and Orthodox, believed for 1900 years until the Lambeth Conference in 1930, and (c) what most of the rest of the world and all the other religions believed until the Sexual Revolution. So you are practicing what C. S. Lewis calls "chronological snobbery" when you dismiss this massive consensus as "beyond the pale of argument". By your account, it seems that everyone in the world, and all Christians in history until 1930, were, like Catholics, "obsessed with sex". That leaves only you and your generation, who are *not* obsessed with sex. I cannot believe that you are really that ignorant, that provincial, or that self-righteous.

I appeal to my example of the teenage drug addict and his parents. Which of the two is obsessed with drugs? Which civilization is obsessed with sex, yours or mine? The new one or the old one? This seems to me to be a very clear case of what the psychologists call projection.

The whole world, before the Sexual Revolution, used to see something sacred about sex. That, rather than theological reasoning, was the basis for all the taboos. You put taboos around the Eucharist, not ordinary bread. You hire police to protect cathedrals, not outhouses. You take care with diamonds, not golf balls. But the very sense of the sacred, the very meaning of that word, is disappearing from the modern consciousness. The word "sacred" now means to most people simply "religious things like Bibles and cathedrals and hymns". That is probably the single most fundamental difference between the old world and the "Brave New World" in which we increasingly live.

I am naïve. I learn slowly. I am surprised when I find how far into "Brave New World" we are. Here is an example: Never in my teaching life did I ever teach a less successful book than Christopher Derrick's *Sex and Sacredness*, which is a very intelligent, well-written defense of the sense of the sacred and then an application of it to sex. No one in my large class "got it".

People who are born color-blind are shocked to learn that others see colors. This discovery that my students were blind to the sense of the sacred was like the shock of discovering that the rest of the world is color-blind.

The same was true about my attempts to teach Peter Shaffer's play *Equus*. The play is about a mentally disturbed boy who worshipped horses and violently blinded them when they watched him have sex and, to his mind, condemned his sin. It was exactly like Nietzsche's self-confessed motive for atheism. He insisted that "God is dead" and that "we killed Him" because we could not live with a God who knows and judges our dark side. In the play, the boy's psychiatrist "cured" him, but he also envied him because he had something to worship, however perverted. The "shrink" shrunk the boy's passion, his worship, his mysticism, and turned him into an ordinary shallow, short-sighted secular social conformist. The play centered on the psychiatrist's dilemma. Only one student out of twenty in my class even had the remotest understanding of why that was a dilemma at all. They instinctively judged that the boy was insane, not just because he blinded horses, but because he worshipped horses, and not just because he worshipped *horses*, but because he *worshipped*. The students even pitied the psychiatrist for having scruples about "curing" him.

Why did all pre-moderns see sex as sacred? Because they saw it as what it is: the natural cause of human life; and they saw life as sacred, as a sacred mystery. Both of these premises are dying or dead. And the most immediate suspect for this murder is The Pill.

The Pill has changed the very essence of sex in our minds. It has replaced sex's objective teleology (end) with our subjective end: it now means pleasure, not children. The pleasure used to be seen as a delightful "accident", in the Aristotelian sense: not something unforeseen and unwanted, but a *property* of the essence rather than the essence; an addition, an extra, like the delicious taste of healthy food. Now procreation is the "accident". "What? Another person? We were not alone on our bed? Our sex made you pregnant with another human being? Impossible! We failed! How terrible! How could it have come to *that*?"

It is not just a question of morality, of the right versus the wrong, but of the religious versus the sacrilegious, of worship versus blasphemy. There is an image that says that. You will not "get" the point of the image unless you believe, as I hope you still do, or at least can remember or imagine yourself believing, as orthodox Catholics do, that the Eucharist is sacred because it is literally God Himself in disguise; that the substance, being, reality, or essence that lies beneath the sensory appearances of the bread and wine, once the priest has consecrated them, is God incarnate, the God-Man Jesus Christ, in His perfect divinity and perfect humanity, and, within that humanity, both body and soul and, within that body, both flesh and blood.

Now here is the image. Imagine a priest who hated and feared Christ but loved the ritual of the Mass. He wanted the rest of the Mass but not Christ's presence. Therefore, he took careful pains to lock the door by which Christ could come and interfere with his pleasure. He lied with his body. He moved his lips but spoke no words at the Consecration. It was like putting a dental dam in his mouth.

That is what contraception does: it deliberately keeps God out, keeps the Creator of new life out of the sexual act that He designed as the most miraculous thing in the world because it co-creates, or procreates, an immortal soul, which is not just part of this world but destined for infinite and eternal life and joy in the next. It says to God: "I reject Your interference, Your miracle, Your creation of a new person, a new image of Yourself, this thing of unique and intrinsic and infinite value. But I want the sex. I want the deed but not the product. I want the pleasure you have attached to this sacred act but not the product of the act. I want the means but not the end. I want the accident but not the essence." This is exactly what the priest wants in his blasphemous fake Mass.

The two most sacred places in the world are the two places where God continually performs miracles that only He can do, in fact, the two greatest of miracles. He creates a new human soul in a woman's body at the moment of biological conception; and He recreates, or transubstantiates, bread and wine into the Body and Blood of His own divine eternal incarnate Son on the altar at a Catholic Mass. The Devil hates those two places above all places on earth. (The next most hated place is that little box where you confess your sins to a priest and are forgiven, where Adam walks in and Christ walks out. The parallel to contraception there would be another lie, where you pretended to repent but didn't, because you didn't want His forgiveness.)

When you put a condom on a penis, you are really intending to put a condom on God. A contraceptive is a padlock on the door of your house to prevent God from entering and doing His creative work.

The Church's No to contraception is not a No to sex but a Yes to sex. The *contraceptive* is the No to sex. It kills sex. For killing is separating body and soul. And contraception does that: it separates the body of sex (the baby) from the soul of sex (the love). It wants the soul but not the body, the spirit but not the matter, the intention of love but not love's body.

Traditionally, sexual intercourse has three natural ends: procreation, intimacy, and pleasure. Even if we assume that the intention in contraception is not just pleasure but loving intimacy, still, it separates the subjective soul of that love from its body. It separates the "unitive meaning" (the love) from the "procreative meaning" (the baby), the subjective from the objective, what-I-personally-want-it-to-be-and-to-mean from what-it-really-is-and-means-in-objective-truth.

I am not claiming this proves that the Church is right. I am just trying to explain what she believes, the "big picture" vision that is behind her No to contraception. You radically misunderstand that vision. You do not have to believe it to understand it. Even an intelligent atheist can understand it, by an exercise of the imagination, though he cannot believe it, since it cannot be true if there is no God.

The Church is not less sexy but far sexier than you are. She loves and values and reverences and praises and almost adores sex. For her, it is not a fun game, but a divine mystery. It is mystical. It knocks your socks off. It knocks you right out of your self, out of your self-control. Contraception insists on bringing this wild horse under your control, putting bit and bridle on it, keeping it confined to the narrow little comfortable trails that you made for it to trot along. You will not let the horse gallop. You demand to make this great thing your servant. You make this wild horse tame.

But that kills it, because part of the essence of the joy of sexual orgasm is the loss of self-control. That is what "ecstasy" means: literally, "standing outside yourself". The two meanings of "ecstatic" ("extremely joyful" and "standing-outside-yourself") are necessarily together. Sex is so ecstatically joyful only because *it bears you away* like a horse. It is a transcendence of the self, a self-forgetful out-of-the-body experience (and an out-of-your-ordinary-mind experience, too). It is like surfing a forty-foot wave.

Contraception means "I give you only part of myself. I hold back my fertility. I'll give you the surface of my sex organ, because that gives me the pleasure, but I won't give you its substance, its depth, the life that is inside it." That's not sexy. It is not a transcendence of self and self-control. It is not the gift of your whole self to the other person. But that gift is what total love is supposed to be. That is why it is supposed to be for life, and with only one person, the total gift of the total self to the other. That otherness is also why it has to be heterosexual.

Did you perhaps tremble on the brink of some affirmation of this vision until I wrote that last word? Which of us is obsessing now? Which of us is ideologically blinkered?

10. Abortion

This is an easy one. I won't go through the obvious argument because I think you understand it. It is a simple syllogism with a moral premise and a factual premise. Its moral premise is that murder (that is, deliberately killing an innocent human being) is morally wrong. Its factual premise is that an unborn human baby is an unborn *human* baby. A zygote or an embryo or a fetus is not another species any more than an infant or a teenager is. It is just another stage of development. The conclusion of the syllogism, the moral wrongness of abortion, necessarily follows from these two premises.

In the early stages of the abortion debate, pro-choicers always denied the second premise. But the scientific facts are so clearly and massively in conflict with that that they usually now deny or nuance the first one—which is a far more radical position and based on a far more radical ignorance: of morality rather than of science. We all know that morality is more important than science. No one, on his deathbed, thinks: "I put too much time and effort into the moral work of being a good person and not enough time and effort into my career of being a good scientist."

I agree with you that we should be both pro-life and pro-choice, that we should "choose life". But what if we don't? What if we want to choose death by killing another person? Should that be allowed for the sake of free choice, or should that be forbidden for the sake of protecting the life of the innocent victim? In all other areas than abortion, the answer is not controversial. Why, then, is it controversial when it comes to abortion? The obvious reason is that abortion is about sex and sexual autonomy. Abortion is emergency contraception.

The essential pro-life argument (in the first paragraph above) still stands, no matter what exceptions and mitigations and psychological motivations and medical complexities and social and family conditions have to be taken into account. They add dimensions to the pro-life argument but do not subtract from it.

Motivation is the main addition, and though it cannot change the gravity of the act, it does change the gravity of the guilt. No one wants to jail women for aborting, and no one wants to say that the personal guilt of the mother, or even the doctor, is the same as that of a Mafia hit man or a terrorist or a Nazi in the Holocaust.

Another addition is political expediency. Almost everyone admits that to preserve social cohesion, many legal and political compromises are necessary. Total reversal of *Roe vs. Wade* tomorrow would probably provoke passionate reactions and riots. Laws and minds should match, so minds must be changed and not just laws.

Most people on both sides agree that education is the road to moral maturity and responsibility, and this actually worked well regarding the rise of environmentalism and the decline of smoking, as well as increased sensitivity to the needs and rights of the handicapped and the attack on the remnants of slavery. I agree with your insistence that the goal must be to get people to "*choose* life" by moral persuasion, not merely to preserve life by force. That means education. And right now, all three of our education establishments, formal education (from kindergarten to university), informal education in the media and journalism, and the entertainment industries, are massively in the hands of the pro-choice abortion establishment.

If you want to work for social justice, if you want to end child abuse, if you want to end the oppression of the weak by the strong, start here by ending the slaughter of our own children. It is the #1 social justice issue of our time. It is the most extreme example of child abuse. And it is the most obvious example of the oppression of the weak by the strong. If fetuses had scalpels and poisons and knives and could fight back against their killers, there would be very few abortions.

And what institution has always stood the firmest and the most unyielding here? Who is the most feared and maligned enemy of the pro-choice establishment? Do you need a hint?

11. Social Justice

The Church, like all the Jewish prophets, has always been big on both collective and individual morality, on both social justice and on individual holiness. (Read the prophet Amos for a good short example.) Alas, most Catholics today are cafeteria Catholics. They are passionate about one of the two dimensions of justice and passive about the other. They call themselves "conservatives" or "liberals", "traditionalists" or "progressives", "right" or "left". It is like the mess in Washington, with neither side of the aisle listening to the other side. One of the worst things that keeps happening to the Church throughout her history is becoming politicized. When religion goes to bed with politics, it discovers that its lover is a tramp.

Orthodox Catholics who think with the Church are passionate about social justice, too, and many sacrifice a lot of time and money and effort in concrete efforts to help the needy, in soup kitchens, homeless shelters, pregnancy help centers, and the like. On the other hand, I don't see many "liberal" Catholics either saying or doing much to foster individual morality or religion, teaching and practicing much prayer, Eucharistic adoration, fasting, etc.

Why is that? One reason is obvious: social justice is popular in our secular society, while individual morality is not, especially when it comes to sex. Social justice is not distinctively Catholic. There are plenty of groups and organizations that work for social justice without any Catholic theology or ecclesiology or even Catholic morality. If that is the whole essence of your religion, there is no reason to be a Catholic. But who else besides Catholics and Evangelicals (and Orthodox Jews) work and speak against the Sexual Revolution and its fruits? We have to work on both areas of the moral battlefield, but we have many allies outside the Church on one field and very few on the other.

The unfortunate notion that you have to choose between *either* social justice *or* traditional Catholic beliefs and values is much more common among "liberals" than among "conservatives". Most "conservative" or "traditional" Catholics I know are actively involved in social justice enterprises, naturally starting with pro-life work (and are in fact far more massively invested in the welfare of mothers and families as well as babies than the other side is), and also in work with the aged, the addicted, the poor, the homeless, etc. But most "social justice" Catholics I know are very light on or openly skeptical of traditional theology, of pro-life work, of devotion to the saints, to personal holiness, to the sacraments, etc. And almost always they are skeptical of traditional Catholic sexual morality. For most of them, social justice seems to be a *substitute* for traditional faith rather than a part of it or a working-out of it. Their view of history always opposes the "enlightened" present to the "unenlightened" past, trashes the past and idealizes the present and the future. Theirs is a "hermeneutic of discontinuity": they see the new (post-Vatican II) stuff as discontinuous with the old. Ironically, this is also true of the very small far right who oppose Vatican II and everything modern. Traditional Catholicism has always embraced the "hermeneutic of continuity", seeing the good new stuff as a natural outgrowth of the good old stuff, like new leaves on the old tree. In contrast, the "progressives" see much "pre-Vatican II stuff" as foreign growths, like barnacles on the ship that have to be scraped off. There's a theological word for that. It's Protestantism.

You say the Church should concentrate on social justice instead of obsessing about individual sexual issues. I have three responses to that. First, who are you to say what Christ's Church should do? If you see the Church as the voice of you rather than the voice of Christ, then you should not call yourself a Catholic at all. Second, the Church's sexual morality is not an "obsession". Modernity's is. The Church thinks with her faith, not with her sex organs. Third, ignoring individual issues for the sake of social issues is a sure way to fail on social issues, because society is only as good as its individuals. You cannot make good houses from bad bricks.

Social justice and individual piety have to go together. There is no way to improve society except by improving individuals, just as there is no way to improve schools except by improving teachers and students. There is also no way to improve individuals without using the societies that socialize and educate them, first of all in their families—which makes the family the first and most important of all social issues. Each pole depends on the other. That is why cafeteria Catholicism harms both poles.

The Church does not give us a cafeteria; she gives us a banquet. She is not an efficient business; she is a Holy Mother. She is not an organization; she is an organism. She is not man's subjective opinions about God, she is God's objective revelation about man. That is the essence of what Catholics believe about her. Leave it or take it, but don't fake it.

12. Traditionalism

In an overly traditional time and culture that is dominated by the old and suspicious of the new, the Church is progressive, even radical. In an overly rebellious time and culture that is dominated by the mentality of teenagers and suspicious of the old, the Church is conservative and traditional. In herself, she is that wise householder who brings out of her storage both the old and the new (Mt 13:52).

"Tradition" means two very different things in Catholic vocabulary. *Human* traditions in the Church are no better or worse, no more or less changeable, than they are anywhere else. But "*Sacred* Tradition" is divine, infallible, and unchangeable in its essence (though not in its expressions or applications) because it comes, not from man, but from God. It is the totality of Christ's teachings handed down (that is what "tradition" literally means) to His apostles, whom He Himself chose and authorized to teach in His name and with His authority. And these apostles (and they alone) ordained successors (called presbyters, bishops, or elders) for the rest of time. That is in the Bible. In Catholic vocabulary, it is called "apostolic succession".

One of the things the apostolic Church did was to write and, later, to canonize (define the content of) the New Testament. So if the apostolic succession and the "Magisterium" (teaching authority) of the Church are only human and fallible, as Protestants believe, and not divine and infallible, as Catholics believe, then neither is the Bible infallible, since a cause cannot give to its effect what it does not have.

Insofar as the Church interacts *politically* with society, she claims infallibility only for her divinely revealed principles, which are very few, and not for the prudence of her practice in applying and living those principles. But even in the past, when she (perhaps unwisely) sided with "throne and altar" (i.e., human traditionalism), she also taught the "liberal" principles of equality, antislavery, freedom, the rights of the poor, and other truths that were not fashionable to the "conservative" political establishments of the past. Similarly, even today, when she embraces modern values like freedoms and rights and equality and democracy, she also teaches ideas like authority and obedience and the value of tradition and the dangers of revolution (especially the Sexual Revolution), ideas that are unfashionable to the modern "liberal" establishment.

If the political systems of the past, such as medieval Christendom, were so dehumanizing and corrupt, as you assume, and if our present political systems are so much better, then why was there so much satisfaction with the old systems and why is there so much dissatisfaction with the new ones? Was everyone just stupid and unenlightened and lacking in current "consciousness-raising" for thousands of years? Was medieval philosophical reasoning inferior to modern versions? Do our philosophers write better Summas than Aquinas'? Was Aquinas' confidence in reason overdone, and is the crisis of reason that is central to most schools of modern philosophers more healthy? Was there more propaganda and ideology and less honest, objective, principled reasoning then or now?

The Church embraces the modern idea of a separation of Church and State today, not because the State would be corrupted by the Church (which is the secularists' fear), but because the Church is usually corrupted by the State. But this prudent separation is not a divinely revealed principle. It is both practically and morally necessary today, in an age of religious pluralism, especially since it seems to be the only alternative to a past that was traumatized by religious wars.

But in principle, the idea of a holy nation, as well as holy individuals, is a thoroughly biblical idea. The Old Testament demands holiness of Gentile nations as well as Israel; and the New Testament continues this demand.

Christian revelation has an essentially social and political dimension. Christianity is not a merely private religion. And this dimension is still alive and well today in the Church's demand for social justice, since the principles of social justice are divinely revealed and part of Sacred Tradition. If you are skeptical of divine revelation and the authority of its Tradition, you weaken your own "liberal" demand for social justice.

Ambrose Bierce, in *The Devil's Dictionary*, defines a conservative as one who is in love with existing evils and a progressive as one who wants to replace these old evils with new ones. Divine revelation has always denounced evils both old and new, both "conservative" and "liberal". Jesus was rejected by both the theological Right (the Pharisees, the "hard line" legalists) and the theological Left (the Sadducees, the anti-supernaturalists, the skeptics).

Christianity is not bound to a political system. In the past, the "throne and altar" traditionalists made that error in tying the Church to conservative regimes; today, it is the "social justice" progressives who make the same error in the opposite direction. Both assume the same false premise: that we can pick and choose what parts of divine revelation to believe. In other words, both are "cafeteria Catholics".

Both also make the same mistake of conflating ideas with persons, heresies with heretics, sins with sinners. Both forget to "hate the sin but love the sinner". The Inquisition tried to abolish sins and heresies by executing sinners and heretics; modern "liberals" try to love sinners and heretics by loving sins and heresies.

The clearest example of this confusion today is the LGBTQ activists. Christians are commanded to love sinners much more (all sinners, both homosexuals and heterosexuals) and sins much less (all sins, both homosexual and heterosexual). Which side today hates and rejects that very distinction?

Jesus was both the tenderest and toughest man who ever lived. Tenderness toward sinners is as much an essential aspect of His authoritative, traditional teaching as toughness toward sins. Catholic theological traditionalism embraces, in principle, both aspects. (Of course *nobody's* practice comes up to his principles unless his principles are as mushy as "have a nice day.") Do "cafeteria Catholics" do the same? Are they tough on sins—all sins—as well as tender to sinners?

13. The "Enlightenment": Science vs. Scientism

The Church's track record on science is excellent. She has supported science and great scientists, e.g., Albert the Great in the thirteenth century and Copernicus in the fifteenth. Copernicus was a priest, like many great scientists, e.g., the inventor of the Big Bang theory in the twentieth century. The Church bankrolled Galileo, and she opposed, not his theory (which was essentially the same as that of Copernicus), but his insistence that it was more than a scientific hypothesis. She did the very same thing with Darwin and evolution in the twentieth century: no problem with the science and the scientific claims, only with the theology of no God, no soul, no design. But that is theology and philosophy, not science. Atheism is a theology, not a science!

The "Enlightenment" was not the beginning of science, nor was it simply the defense of science. It was a philosophy: it was the invention of the fake "war between Science and Religion"; it was the idea that science contradicted and disproved religion—which it never did. If you want to talk about "the war between Science and Religion", tell me which dogma of religion, correctly and theologically defined, has been disproved by which discovery, correctly and scientifically defined, of which science. No one has ever answered that question. Instead, two vague and unreal abstractions have been pitted against each other: "religion" and "science". This "phony war" has zero casualties. Be scientific! Don't substitute popular ideological clichés for scientific data.

The Church has always contained some fools, like the bishops who refused to look though Galileo's telescope and the fundamentalists who believe in a 6000-year-old earth because they don't know science and also misinterpret the Bible. Such fools are also occasionally to be found in the Senate, the YMCA, the Harvard Alumni Association, and the Masons; why not argue that those organizations, too, are anti-science?

No stronger philosophical basis for science has ever been propounded than Christian theology, with its intelligent God intelligently designing an intelligible world and giving man the power of human intelligence, which is part of His own image in the human soul, to investigate and discover and understand the world. Many non-religious scientists (like Einstein) have been deeply impressed by, and have strongly affirmed the existence of, a "cosmic intelligence" behind the elegant laws of the physical and biological worlds.

If you believe that "science contradicts religion", you must either reject one of the two or reject logic and embrace contradictory beliefs. I do not think you are irrational enough to be an enemy of logic, and you do not seem to be an enemy of science, so why doesn't that make you an enemy of religion, especially the oldest and most formidable one? Why don't you call yourself an anti-Catholic instead of a cafeteria Catholic?

Perhaps your next paragraph is your answer. You say you have a quarrel, not with religion, but with "organized religion". But not with "spirituality".

14. "Spirituality" vs. "Organized Religion"

You say you "have no quarrel with spirituality". Well, I do.

If you defend "spirituality" *instead* of religion, you are repeating the old heresy of Gnosticism, which confuses the distinction between spirit and matter with the distinction between good and evil, or Godly and ungodly.

But this is refuted by two things: (1) the greatest sins are all spiritual sins, especially pride and hypocrisy, and (2) the most evil beings in all reality are pure spirits: demons, devils, fallen angels. According to all three Western religions, all matter is good. God said so when He created it.

What does it mean to worship God because He is spirit rather than to worship Him because He is good? It means to worship spirit as such, and therefore your own spirit, soul, or self. Chesterton calls this "spirituality" "a dreadful doom". He says, "Let him worship anything but that. Let him worship crocodiles, if he can find any in his street, but let him not worship the Inner Light, because that means worshipping himself."

That is not the definition of worship; it is the definition of Hell. Some of the great mystics say that they do not believe there is material fire in Hell because that would be something other than the self, and in Hell there is nothing other than the self, there is just the self, alone forever in total loneliness. Fire hurts, but fire is beautiful and designed and created by God, and therefore it is good in some way. But there is no goodness in Hell. There is only the self, which has rejected the other, God and the world and the other people that God created. The whole point of life is to get you *out* of yourself and your "original selfishness" into which you are born. That is what love (*agape*, altruism, charity) does. Infants, like animals, are inherently selfish. Of course, we don't blame them because their free will has not yet emerged. But we do socialize them out of it.

An associated meaning of "spirituality" is "spiritualism", the occult, some sort of supernatural technology, contacting dead souls. I am pretty sure you do not mean that. And you probably do not mean Gnosticism, either (spirit = good, matter = evil). You probably mean simply suspicion of the visible institutional Church.

In many senses, I share your suspicion. The Church has approved some stupid things policy-wise, like the Inquisition; and her clergy have done some horribly wicked things, like seducing altar boys and seminarians; and even some of her popes (the Borgias) have been positively and spectacularly wicked. But not officially, not by following her Magisterium, her Sacred Tradition, her divinely authorized teaching authority, but always by contradicting it. They made that Tradition stand out all the more clearly by violating it. None of the bad popes ever changed the rules. God had said that sex and women and children and the poor are sacred objects to be revered, not used or put down; and when bad popes and bishops violated them, they never changed God's rules to excuse their sins. They were hypocrites: they did not practice what they preached; but they kept preaching it. (Actually, technically, a hypocrite is one who does not *believe* what he preaches. But I use the term in the popular sense.) Matthew Arnold said that "hypocrisy is the tribute that vice pays to virtue." The evil popes and bishops and priests (who have always been with us, from Judas Iscariot to Cardinal McCarrick) were hypocrites who failed to practice what they preached, but they were not Machiavellians who changed what they preached to conform to their practice.

So yes, the Church is a ship of fools, but she is not a foolish ship. Noah's family on the Ark may have been incompetent sailors, yet the Ark is the ark of salvation. God designed it. It is the divine design of the ship that is holy, not the sailors. And even among the sailors, you find great saints as well as great sinners. Show me another institution that produces as many saints, as much wisdom and holiness in every age. Did you ever actually read the saints? Or do you trust what sinners write about saints instead of what saints write about sinners?

Jesus did not prefer "spirituality" to religion. When He said "the kingdom of God is within you", He certainly did not mean to teach Gnosticism. Both good *and* evil are within us to begin with, in our hearts and motives, and both are also in that part of the material world that is the work of our hands and that manifests our hearts. (Also, in that saying of Jesus, the Greek word for "within" here could also mean "among".)

If Jesus was "spiritual", why did He perform physical miracles? Why did He institute the Eucharist? Why did He have to die? And why did He have to resurrect physically?

15. Jesus

You say: "I say Yes to Jesus, that is why I say No to the Church." No you don't.

You do not say Yes to the real Jesus, the Jesus of history, the Jesus of the Gospels (did you ever actually read the four Gospels?), the Jesus who claims to be your Lord and God and Savior, and not just one of millions of nice guys or "the man for others". How lame and wimpy! Why would anyone bother either to crucify or to worship that?

Jesus wants to change you into a version of Himself. You respond by changing Him into a version of yourself. You say that "heretics and modernists" are closer to "the spirit of Christ" than the Church is. So what is that "true spirit of Christ"? Is it different from what the Church has always taught as divine revelation, as the actual teachings of Jesus as handed down by Sacred Tradition, including the New Testament? If not, then you are not a "cafeteria Catholic" but a non-Catholic. If so, then "the true spirit of Christ" can be nothing but your alternative gospel, your deconstruction and reconstruction of the historical Christ, which turns out to be some set of pious words that you use to express your personal beliefs, which come from your preferences and likes and interests and comforts. God sends you mail that is full of blood, and you clean and polish and edit it. You turn blood into psychobabble. He turned water into wine, and you do the same miracle in reverse. He gives you the Church Militant, and you turn her into Mister Rogers' Neighborhood.

I think I know why. The key word in your argument is the word "was". You say that "Jesus was the man for others" as if He were dead. If there is any one belief that defines Christianity, it is that He is alive. He is risen. Not just "rose" but "is risen". Present tense. You can meet Him. He can *do things to you*, and not just like other good dead people, through your own memory, but through His Real Presence and power. That is the biggest difference between your Jesus and mine. It is not ideological. It is not just that your Jesus is pop psychology plus the Democratic Party platform, while mine is more interesting. It is that yours is dead, and mine is alive.

That is why you call the Mass "a beautiful ritual". If I wanted beautiful rituals, I would go to a hundred other places: symphony orchestras and dance ensembles and basketball games and operas and performances of Shakespeare, or just a walk in the woods and on the beach. The Mass as secular art cannot compare with them. What makes it great is His Real Presence, not its entertainment value. If you want loud, contemporary entertainment, go Baptist and "express yourself" with "praise choruses" and "Christian rock". On second thought, that is at least as insulting to rock as it is to Christianity. So just go to a rock concert, for Nat's sake.

The Catholics who are leaving the Church because she does not "meet their needs" are confusing their needs with their wants. What they really need is the real Christ; what they really need is salvation from their sin; what they really need is to become saints. That is what the real Christ says. (Read the Book!) But what they want is something more comforting, like cliches and a pat on the head and a hug and permission to live by their own rules sexually (that is almost always the bottom line once you do some digging into their lives and hearts). But they don't want to pay a hundred dollars an hour to a psychiatrist for it.

But going to the Church for that kind of uplift is like going to a volcano for some hot air.

Believing a religion is not buying a product, it is accepting an operation. You apparently just do not believe the "bad news" of the x-ray.

You know who Jesus said you were like? The Pharisees! Your favorite villains. Read Luke 5:27–32. Don't blame me for saying that. I didn't write the book.

Have I insulted you yet? You almost certainly think so. Yet I have really done the opposite: I have too much respect for your mind *not* to insult those second-hand unoriginal platitudes you peddle as unworthy of you.

Let's center on the center. Everything else is peripheral; this is central and essential. Everything else is about the teachings of the Lord; this is about the Lord. Who is your Lord: Jesus or yourself? Is He your Savior from your sins or not? I have labeled you a Protestant a few times in this letter. I now take that back. Evangelical Protestants clearly know the answer to that question. You apparently do not.

Well, I may have lost you with those insults, but at least I got your attention.

16. Ecumenism

You say you are a Catholic because you were born into this religion. Not true. No one gets to be a member of His Body by physical birth, only by what Jesus Himself calls the "new birth", or being "born again" spiritually, by "water and the Spirit" (Jn 3:3, 5), i.e., by faith and baptism.

So being a Catholic is just a matter of family loyalty for you? Suppose you were born into a family of Nazis or Satanists. Would you accept the label out of loyalty? Don't you have the gumption to make your own personal choice? You talk a lot about freedom, but you do not seem to practice it much.

All religions are equal, you say. But you think that some (your cafeteria Catholicism) are more equal than others (my orthodox Catholicism), right? That is Orwellian "Newspeak"!

You use the popular image of different religions being different roads up the same mountain. If what you mean by that is that all religions are our attempts to climb into the spiritually higher elevations, into something more Godlike, into more truth, goodness, and beauty, I agree with the goal but not with the assumption that all the roads are roads up, from us, from the bottom. For that assumes that religion is only man's search for God. Even *that* is a great thing, and I think you are right in seeing that since all humans are essentially equal, the human basis for all religions that are roads up the mountain is essentially equal, since we all begin at the same base (though obviously each one has an emphasis or an insight that makes it distinctive, too). That is true of all religions except one. All of them are man's search for God, but one of them is God's search for man. How could man's search for God be equal to God's search for man?

C. S. Lewis says that talking about "man's search for God" is like talking about "the mouse's search for the cat". How could the road God made down the mountain be equal to the many roads man makes up the mountain? Christianity, like Judaism before it (and Islam after it), claims to be God's invention, not man's. Many ways up the mountain are indeed made by man, but one way down was made by the person who said "I am the way, and the truth, and the life; no one comes to the Father, but by me" (Jn 14:6). If that claim is not true, then that man is the most intolerant, arrogant, proud, blasphemous, sacrilegious, egotistic, or insane false prophet who ever lived. Neither Moses nor Muhammad nor Buddha nor Lao Tzu nor Confucius ever claimed to be God in the flesh! But if that claim *is* true, then His road (which is Himself) is no more equal to other roads than He is equal to you, for God is not equal to man.

And the claim about the Catholic Church is like the claim about Christ. If Jesus is not the Christ, He is the Antichrist, and if the Church is not His church, it is the Antichrist's favorite denomination.

Your last sentence says: "We should be tolerant and respectful of the roads, except for the one that is intolerant and disrespectful of all the others." I think you are implying here that the Catholic Church is "the one that is intolerant and disrespectful of all the others." But that is simply not true. One of the things the Catholic Church teaches is that there are profound truths in all religions, that we should learn from them, and that even where they are wrong, we should be tolerant and respectful of people who hold erroneous ideas, though not of the ideas themselves. Did you ever actually read the documents of Vatican II?

Also, the Church's claim to exclusivity is not a claim about the Catholic religion but a claim about Christ. And even that claim is not exclusive but universal (the literal meaning of "catholic"), for the New Testament describes the *Logos*, the Word or Mind of God, the pre-incarnate Christ, as "the true light that enlightens every man [who] was coming into the world" (Jn 1:9). It does not limit the knowledge of the true God to Christians. Saint Justin Martyr, in the second century, called Socrates a Christian for that reason. And Erasmus prayed, "Saint Socrates, pray for us." That is what you call intolerance and disrespect?

Only one woman in the world is my wife; does that mean I disrespect other women? Only one man is my father; does that mean I disrespect all other men? I see in other women, from afar, some of the same beautiful things I see in my wife. And I see in other men, from afar, the same fatherly virtues I see in my father. And I see in other religions, from afar, some of the same truth, goodness, and beauty that I see in the Catholic Church. The more I appreciate the Church, the more I appreciate other religions as well.

17. Sacramentalism

You say you label yourself a Catholic because you love the Church's good works and her sacraments. Every good man loves every good work of every other good man and institution, so that is not at all distinctive. But the Catholic Church is distinctive in her sacraments. So let's talk about them.

You say "I do not believe I have to sign every line of an arcane and archaic creed in order to (have the right to) receive them (the sacraments)." But you do.

It is a kind of "truth in labeling". Let me try to explain. The sacraments are "sacred signs" (that is the meaning of the word). What are they "signs" of? Of two things: of God's presence and activity in them and of your freely chosen faith in them. The "arcane and archaic creeds" simply define your faith, define what your faith is faith in. Simply having faith is not enough; it might be faith in Charles Manson, Adolf Hitler, Satan, or a god with a dark side. The creeds are not arcane but simple and clear, and they are not archaic because, like the formulas of science, they express changeless objective truths.

For instance, if you do not believe that Jesus is the Son of God and the Savior, then you are lying with your body when you receive the sacrament of the Eucharist. That word "eucharist" literally means "thanks", or "thanksgiving". Thanks for what? For your salvation. From whom? From Him. Not from Moses or Buddha or Muhammad.

And if you do not believe that Christ gave his chosen apostles and their successors the authority to forgive sins, as the Gospels say He did, then you should not go to confession to a Catholic priest to get your sins forgiven. That is just honesty. Priests are priests of Christ, not free psychologists with a quick fix. What they offer you, in the sacraments, is the very life (not just "life-style") of Jesus Christ. That is what begins in baptism and is strengthened in confirmation, and is nourished in the Eucharist, and is restored in confession. If you do not believe in that Person and in the claim that you can be given a share in His supernatural life, and that the sacraments do that, then please do not lie and say that you do believe that by receiving the sacraments.

There is nothing nasty or narrow there. It is just honesty. If you do not believe in capitalism, do not invest in the stock market. If you do not believe in the unconscious, do not go to a Freudian psychoanalyst. If you do not believe in the Constitution, do not seek American citizenship. If you are not a meat eater, look for a vegetarian restaurant. If you do not want the heat, get out of the sun. If you are not married to x, do not have sex with x. These are all signs, signatures, testimonies, witnesses, oaths. Do not swear false oaths. Not because you would hurt or pollute the Church but because you would hurt and pollute your own conscience and honesty and innocence. I am not saying: "get out of my Church"; I am saying: "Examine your conscience and your faith inwardly before you profess it outwardly."

By the way, all my snarky-sounding and "judgmental" critiques are meant to challenge you, not to condemn you; to elicit from you the response: "You judge me unfairly. I do believe all that stuff that you believe."

18. Death

You want a Catholic funeral. Good, but I hope you know what that means. A funeral is not essentially a celebration of the past life of the dead person. We do not celebrate at death; we mourn! A funeral, like any Church service, is vertical, not just horizontal; its essence is a prayer, not just a collective memory, a community of connections between the people at the funeral through their memories of the dead person. Even atheists have that kind of funeral.

A Catholic funeral is a public and communal prayer to God for the dead person, a committing him to God for eternity. If you do not believe in a God who hears and answers prayers, or if you do not believe in life after death and Heaven and what the Church teaches about how to get there, then your desire for a Catholic funeral is as meaningless as art from an artist who does not believe there is such a thing as beauty, morality from someone who does not believe there really is such a thing as moral goodness, or philosophy from a philosopher (literally, a "lover of wisdom") who does not believe that there is any such thing as wisdom.

You are certainly right to say, echoing the words of Christ, that just as the Sabbath was made for man, not man for the Sabbath, so the Church was made for man, not man for the Church. But since the Sabbath was made for man, therefore if one does not observe the Sabbath, then its purpose for man is thwarted and frustrated. The same is true with the Church. It is like Noah's Ark (a biblical parallel, not mine). The Ark is made for man, not man for the Ark. It is like a life raft. But if you don't get aboard the Ark, if you don't conform your thoughts and actions to what that thing actually is—a real life raft, not an idea or an ideology or an abstraction or a work of your own art or of your own thought—then it cannot do its work for you, and you will not be saved from the flood.

No, I am not saying that non-Catholics go to Hell. The Church herself condemned that idea. To say that Christ is the only Savior and that the Church is His only "mystical body" is not to judge who is saved or who are members of that body. The Church is invisible as well as visible, and the first is larger than the second.

You want a Catholic funeral because you know how important death is. That is wise. Death is the supreme test of life, of man, of honesty, and of faith. Of life, because at death the whole of one's life is complete, like a book that is finished and goes home to the printer. Of man, because it is man as a whole who dies and apparently ceases to exist. (But does he? "To be or not to be, that is the question" at death.) Of honesty, because it is almost impossible to lie to yourself and to God when you are facing death; it forces the truth out of you. Of faith, because only a faith that is stronger than death, only a faith that can conquer death, is worth bothering with. All other faiths are just dreams. They pop out of existence like bubbles or fog when the light of morning comes.

There are two different kinds of death. Physical death is the death of the body. Sin is the death of the soul. Jesus came to save us from both kinds of death, since body and soul are one substance, one entity, not two. The whole point of the Catholic faith, the whole point of the Catholic Church, is to plug us into Jesus the Savior from death. That is the point of all the creeds and all the Commandments and all the sacraments. The creeds are a road map for your mind, and the Commandments are a GPS for your car, and the sacraments are food for your journey. And all these things, everything in Catholicism, are tested and proved at death.

That is the strongest reason to embrace the Church. If you never had to die, you could procrastinate and experiment and keep going in and out of every religion again and again forever. In fact, you could be a "cafeteria Catholic". But if "it is a matter of life or death", you had damn well better eat the food of immortality, especially when it is offered to you by a God who knows you, loves you, designed you, created you, and wants you to come Home to enjoy Him forever. As soon as you know you are going to die and as soon as you know that you do not know when, the time has come to stop playing games and get serious.

19. Inclusivism

"Catholic" means "universal", and "universal" means "all-inclusive". But what sorts of things are being referred to here when you praise "inclusivism". Ideas? Impossible; some ideas exclude others. Values? Same thing. What the Church "includes" is all human beings, all God's children, created in His image, destined for Heaven. Her ministry is to everyone. Her "big tent" is the biggest tent.

She is "diverse". But truth is not "diverse". Surely you don't believe that literally stupid and silly notion that "what's true for you is not necessarily true for me"; that there is no such thing as a universal human nature that we all share; or that human nature is so "diverse" that there can be no basic moral principles that are based on universal human nature.

You cannot have inclusivism without exclusivism. You have to exclude falsehoods in order to include truths. You have to be intolerant to what is false and harmful to human happiness if you are going to be on the side of what is true and helpful to human happiness. And you have to be absolute ("fanatical") about the two absolutes that stem from the very eternal nature of God, namely, truth and love.

All religions have three aspects, often called creed, code, and cult (or culture); or words, works, and worship. They appeal to the three most basic aspects of the human soul: mind, will, and heart. God is the origin and object of all three: the revealer of truths that we could not come to know by our own power, the giver of laws that direct us better than we could direct ourselves, and the inventor of forms of worship, both public and private, that fulfill us and help us enter into that supernatural life, that union with God, which is our final end and highest joy.

God's religion has to be better than ours! We are like foolish children who want to believe only what our own minds have discovered, not what others who are wiser have told us; who want to live by the rules of our own easy games rather than learning to play adult games; and who want to eat foods that taste sweet rather than foods that make us healthy.

The third aspect, worship, follows the same pattern as the other two. So your joke about worshipping God in your own way is really funny, but the joke is on you.

20. Hope

Our hopes differ. Yours centers on a church remade in the image of spiritual children, "re-formed" in our image, rather than by reforming ourselves in the image of our Creator and Designer. This is the essence of idolatry, which is forbidden by "the first and greatest commandment". Idolatry means divinizing a creature and creaturizing God, exalting what is not God (for instance, an ideology) to the place of our absolute, our God, and also chopping God down to our size, making Him in our image instead of letting Him make us in His. (One wag said that God created us in His own image, and we have been returning Him the favor ever since.) If you have a religion that is "updated" in accordance with human fashions, it is going to be as changeable as the wind or the waves that undermine all our sand castles. If you want to see your "cafeteria Catholicism", go to the beach.

Our hopes differ. Your hope is in man; mine is in God. Your hope is yourself and people who think like you. Mine is in God's apostles and prophets, who think God's thoughts.

Honestly, Nat, don't you feel a little arrogant and foolish in telling God where to get off? And if it is *not* God who speaks through Christ and His Church, then it is not you but the Church that is being insufferably arrogant (and the same goes for Christ), and you should denounce it as the work of the Devil. For pride was the Devil's essential sin.

The Church does not need you, Nat. You need her. She

does not need you to reform her. You need her to reform you. And so do I need her to reform me.

Rereading this long letter to you, I see frequent impatience and preachiness and insensitivity in it. Why? Because I judge myself by the mind of the Church, which is "the mind of Christ" (Phil 2:5; 1 Cor 2:16). All I am asking from you is to do the same.

PART THREE

Critique of Kreeft's

"Either/Or Thinking"

by Nat Whilk

After sending my long response letter to Nat and receiving his permission to publish it, I got a second suggestion from him shortly after: that we try to focus our differences on a single all-embracing difference, which Nat called "either/or thinking". I agreed, because I thought there was, indeed, one single pattern to all our differences and that that was it; but what Nat judged a fallacy, I judged a virtue. So this second stage of our debate seemed to both of us to be the center of it all, the nub and hub and rub. When Shakespeare has Hamlet say, in his most famous soliloquy, "Aye, there's the rub", he means "There's the catch." A catch on a door is a latch: if it is shut, the door blocks entrance; if it is open, it invites entrance. Nat thinks "either/or thinking" is a "catch" that blocks his full entrance into the Church. I think it opens up a clear path into her.

Critique of Kreeft's
"Either/Or Thinking"

Dear Dr. Kreeft,

Although we did not come to agreement about any of the points in my article defending my "cafeteria Catholicism", I think we did make progress in identifying the issues, clarifying them, and focusing our differences on a single kind of thinking that you use in nearly all of your responses and which I am deeply suspicious of. (Ending a sentence with a preposition like that is something up with which editors will not put.) I call it "either/or thinking", or "black-and-white thinking". Many textbooks in informal logic identify this as a logical fallacy.

For instance, if one person acts in an apparently bizarre manner (e.g., throwing himself into a thorn bush or an icy river, as Saint Francis is said to have done), an observer may say that his acts were either "from God or from the Devil", and that he needed either to be canonized as a saint or exorcised as demon-possessed. I would say, on the other hand, that most likely he is neither, but merely a well-intentioned holy man who is so overly humble as to be masochistic and who deserves neither worship nor exorcism but psychoanalysis.

Your defense of religion in general, of monotheism, of Judaism, of Christianity, and of orthodox Catholicism all fits this same pattern. It is understandable and even forgivable in a beginner, but not in a professional philosopher, especially one who has written a textbook on logic!

This "black or white fallacy" is similar to the "slippery slope fallacy". For instance, in some of your other books, you attack abortion rights by arguing that once we grant abortion we are "on the slippery slope" to infanticide, involuntary euthanasia, and eventually genocide. This is simply not true. Historically, there are many examples of cultures that approve abortion but not infanticide (e.g., contemporary America and Europe) or infanticide but not genocide (e.g., ancient Greece and Rome). Perhaps all three are evil, perhaps not, but they are clearly not the same.

The fallacy originates in feeling and substituting it for clear logical thinking. First, some act is strongly felt to be evil, and then other acts that "feel" similar to it are associated with it and declared evil as well. But "evil" is highly ambiguous, and ambiguities can be detected only by thought, not by feeling. There is moral evil and physical evil, and they are very different. And among moral evils, there are public and private evils, harms done to the community and harms done to oneself, and they are different. And among harms, there are harms to one's body, one's mind, one's feelings, or one's freedoms, and they are different. And different things must be dealt with in different ways. Distinctions must be made. Abortion simply is not infanticide, euthanasia, or genocide. It is different in kind, not merely in degree; in quality, not merely in quantity. It is a different kind of act.

When we talk about any concrete reality, we are talking about something multi-dimensional and complex. This applies both to an act like abortion and to a concrete institution like the Catholic Church. In other words, concrete things are like cafeterias. They are made of many parts. They offer many products. The reasonable thing to do in a cafeteria is to make relative value judgments, to choose steak one day and fish the next, or soup for an appetizer and a sandwich for the main course.

It is reasonable, therefore, to be "judgmental", to be a discriminating eater, and not either a non-discriminating baby who eats all the baby food Mommy puts on his plate or an equally non-discriminating anorexic whose attitude toward all foods is fear and loathing.

Religion in general, and the Catholic religion in particular, has a deeply mixed track record. It has immensely helped mankind cope with its most fundamental problems of finding meaning in life, in suffering, in death, in love, and in human relationships. It has also encouraged and justified hate, oppression, self-righteousness, wars, and witch hunts, and it has stifled free inquiry, self-esteem, self-expression, and human happiness. To deny either of these two empirical facts is either to be willfully blind (which is a moral fault) or to be a victim of "either/or thinking" (which is an intellectual fault). I accuse you, Dr. Kreeft, of the lesser evil, the intellectual fault. For I want to practice your own principle of being non-judgmental to persons and judgmental to their ideas.

Sincerely yours,
Your friend,
Nat Whilk

PART FOUR

Response

by Peter Kreeft

Dear Nat,

I thank you for your continued friendship with me, which I value very highly, even though you see me as deeply flawed logically. I feel exactly the same way toward you, and I hope we continue our friendship and active association and communication. It is very important to have friends who do not pat you on the back but kick you in the pants. It keeps you alert and moving.

I will first defend my "either/or thinking" in general and then justify my applying it to the five issues you list: religion, monotheism, Judaism, Christianity, and Catholicism.

As you no doubt clearly know, logic has three parts, based on the three "acts of the mind": conceiving (or understanding), judging, and reasoning.

Reasoning means deriving one truth (the conclusion) from other truths (the premises) either by deductive reasoning, which proves its conclusion with certainty, or inductive reasoning, which gives it more or less probability. Reasoning is either valid (no fallacies) or invalid (fallacious). In valid reasoning, the conclusion necessarily follows (either certainly or probably) from its premises; in fallacious reasoning, not so.

Reasoning thus presupposes judging: judging that the premises are true. Premises are propositions. Propositions are either true or false; there is no third possibility halfway between truth and falsity, just as there is no third possible kind of reasoning that is halfway between valid and invalid. (We can know the truth of the conclusion of a valid deductive argument with certainty if the premises are all true; there are, of course, infinitely variable degrees of probability in induction.)

So two of the three acts of the mind are either/ors. But

in the other act, the "first act of the mind", as you rightly point out, we must avoid either/or thinking, or black and white thinking. This is where logic is rightly "fuzzy". Thus the proposition "the Church is holy" can be true in one sense and false in another, depending on what you mean by "holy" (how holy?) and what you mean by "the Church" (her people are human fools and sinners, but her dogmas are divinely revealed truths and laws).

Take the definition of monotheism: "God is one", or "There is only one God." That is true only if you mean by "God" something other than what pagan polytheists mean and only if "one" does not necessarily exclude some kind of plurality within its oneness. For instance, Trinitarians (Christians) are monotheists (only one God) even though they say God is three Persons, not only one.

Furthermore, no one fully understands any one of the three words in that little definition: "God", "one", or "is". Remember Bill Clinton's lawyer-sneaky but philosophically accurate defense: "It all depends on what you mean by 'is'."

So I quite agree with your attack on "either/or thinking" about real things like the Church. I myself had some very nasty things to say about her, things that many "non-cafeteria Catholics" would find shocking. The prophets (*God's* prophets!) had many similarly nasty things to say about God's chosen people and their priests in the Old Testament. But that did not mean that God's visible institution (Israel) was not God's institution or that God's laws were not God's laws or that God's prophets were not God's prophets.

Similarly, the Church's human sins and follies do not mean that her dogmas and laws are not divine. Or that the claim, the proposition, the dogma that they are divine and not just human is neither true nor false. Once the terms are clarified and freed from ambiguity, a proposition is either true or false. Once the two sides mean the same thing by the words—for instance, the word "God" as used by a theist and by an atheist—they really do contradict each other, and "either/or" thinking is required. Once Romeo proposes to Juliet, she can say only Yes or No, she cannot say Yo. She can wobble like a yo-yo between Yes and No, but she cannot create a third answer. She can only avoid giving either one. And we have the same limited options to God's spiritual marriage proposal as Juliet has to Romeo's.

To use a related analogy: you cannot be half pregnant. You can, however, be five minutes pregnant or five months pregnant. Thus, the thief on the cross was five minutes pregnant with *zoe*, the divine life offered by Christ, while Mother Teresa may be five decades pregnant with *zoe* and so advanced in it that she is in no need of any Purgatory. That is a matter of degree, a "gray" rather than a black or white. But you either do or do not have *zoe*, divine life, Christ's divine life, in your soul. That is either black or white, darkness or light, whether the light is tiny or great. You may not *know* you have it—you may be what Karl Rahner called an "anonymous Christian" (e.g., Socrates, or Emeth in *The Last Battle*), but you either do or do not have it.

And Christ's claim to be the only-begotten Son of God —that is either true or false. Our understanding of what it means is not an either/or, not black or white. It is always some kind of gray, some mixture of understanding and misunderstanding. (But what is gray but a mixture of black and white?)

There is room for fuzzy logic, or grays (in the "first act of the mind") and also room for either/or logic (in the other two acts of the mind). So it is I who am the more inclusive here, for my logic includes yours, but yours excludes mine. I have a place for your fuzzy logic, but you have no place for my either/or logic. It is you who confuse the two. It is I who distinguish them. We need either/or logic to distinguish "either/or logic" from "both/and logic" or "fuzzy logic".

This is all very abstract and theoretical, but I strongly suspect it all comes down to sex in our sex-obsessed culture today. "Binary" (another term for "either/or") is a bad word for transsexuals. They don't *feel* "binary". But how you feel is no index of how things really are. Objectively and scientifically, there are only two genders and only two sex hormones. But in our thinking and feeling, there are no fewer than 54 genders, according to the latest fashion statement from Canada. There are, indeed, men who feel like women, but they are not women, they are men who feel like women. There is, indeed, a great variety of sexual feelings and thinkings and identifyings, subjectively, but only two sexual identities objectively. As propositions are either true or false, humans are either male or female; but within each there are many shades of gray. Our understanding of every term (except perhaps numbers) is a matter of grays, more or less, better or worse. The glass is always partly full and partly empty. It is indeed "the black or white fallacy" to claim total, simple, clear, and adequate understanding of any term. But it is not "the black or white fallacy" to claim to know the truth or falsity of a proposition. Once the known ambiguities of the terms are avoided and once the two sides of a debate can agree about the meaning of the terms (the first act of the mind), we can then give valid or invalid reasons (the third act of the mind) for believing that a proposition (the conclusion, the second act of the mind) is true or false.

And we do not need *total* understanding in order to have agreement about the meaning of terms and to proceed then to logical debate, for we *never* have total understanding, but we sometimes do have agreement about meanings.

And the rules of the logical debate that proceeds are black or white logical rules, because every proposition, once freed from ambiguity, is either true or false, and every deductive argument is either logically valid or invalid. Those two things are black or white but not fallacious.

"Religion is good", "God is good", "The Catholic Church is good"—these are all highly ambiguous propositions because there are senses of "good" that make them all true, and there are senses of "good" that make them all false. But once those different senses are distinguished, the proposition is either true or false. Even for Christ. He was not good in some senses: He was not a good shot with a rifle, a good (i.e., comforting and satisfying) pop psychologist, or a good (effective, successful) propagandist and liar.

We do not have to understand fully the terms "apple", "fruit", and "vegetable" to know that the proposition "Apples are vegetables, not fruits" is either true or false. We do not have to understand fully the terms (like "only-begotten Son of God" or "divine") to understand that the Church's claim for Christ, that He is the only-begotten Son of God (which is simply Christ's claim for Himself), is either true or false. That is not "the black or white fallacy", that is just logic and common sense.

So here are my five basic arguments:

First, about the broadest meaning of "religion": either

there is or is not some "Higher Power" (AA's vague but useful term for what is common to all religions) that is greater than humanity and to which we owe acknowledgment and admiration and aspiration. If That exists, It is the most important thing, the greatest thing. If not, belief in It is the greatest illusion or superstition or myth.

Second, about the personality and will of this Higher Power. Either It is a Person, with a will and, therefore, commandments, laws, or values, or not. Either It is amoral or moral. Either It is the God of the Jews or the God of pantheism, "beyond good and evil", Shiva the destroyer as well as Vishnu the creator. The God of Judaism, Christianity, and Islam has no "dark side", as the God of Hindu, Buddhist, Taoist, or "Star Wars" pantheism does. Either the divine sanction behind human conscience exists and is both personal and absolute, or not. Either morality goes all the way up or not; either conscience is God's prophet in the soul, or it is only human. And that difference is immense.

Third, either Jesus is the divine Son of God or not. If so, all ought to fall down and worship Him. If not, He deserves either a padded cell and a straitjacket (if He actually believed this ridiculous falsehood), or else, if He did not believe it but deliberately lied to deceive us and elicit our false worship and obedience, He deserves crucifixion if anyone ever did, or at least imprisonment without parole, or at least the strongest moral condemnation as a liar and the most severe religious reprobation as an idolater.

Fourth, the Catholic Church either is or is not the one visible church Christ founded and invested with His divine authority as the instrument of His continued presence, teaching, practicing, and spiritually ruling human hearts and lives until the end of time. If she is, well, then, she is; and if she is not, then she is an arrogant false prophet claiming "Thus says the Lord" for merely human opinions and decisions. As Jesus is either the best of men or the worst of men, the Catholic Church is either the best of churches or the worst.

Fifth, this Church, in both her Eastern ("Orthodox") and Western ("Catholic") branches, has priests that claim to be the instruments God has chosen to change bread and wine into the Body and Blood of Christ in the Eucharist to feed mankind with Christ's own supernatural life. If that claim is true, it is far and away the greatest thing in the world. If it is false, it is the world's greatest blasphemy, idolatry, and hoax.

I do not see how any honest, clear-thinking person can avoid these either/ors. God Himself designed them to be like swords, piercing hearts and minds and forcing choices that are demanding and uncomfortable—like Romeo inviting Juliet to marry him and trust him with her life.

By the way, the traditional sexual imagery is neither irreverent nor chauvinist. It is not made in the image of human sex; human sex is holy because it is made in the image of it. And it is not male chauvinism to call God "He" (as 100 percent of Jewish, Christian, and Muslim scriptures and traditions have always done) because it means we are all "she" to Him. He impregnates us, not we Him. He Himself, in both Bible and Church, uses the imagery of our horizontal relationship between equals (from the beginning, "the image of God" is identified, not as male, but as equally "male and female") as an image of the vertical relationship between unequals, the divine and the human.

I don't claim to know, but I strongly suspect, that your reluctance to embrace the logical either/or argument is strongly influenced by your suspicion of this old "sexist" imagery and relationship. I suspect that to you it makes both God and humanity too "sexy". I suspect that sexual analogy and imagery is to you both irreverent to God and over-reverent to man and human sexuality. You want a sexless, purely spiritual, religion. But God gave us another kind.

And if sex is indeed an icon, an aspect of the very "image of God", then that is why sex is the most interesting thing in life, the hardest thing to tame and control, the source of our most passionate happiness and unhappiness, and the only real rival to religion.

You are probably thinking one of three things now.

1. Perhaps you are thinking: "I never thought of that. You have planted doubts in my mind. I shall have to think about that and make some hard choices."

2. Or perhaps you are thinking: "You had me going there for a bit, so logical did you sound. But now I see that you are hopelessly trapped in old sexual stereotypes. The cat is out of the bag. I don't need conversion; you need psychoanalysis. You are a dinosaur. Your kind is becoming extinct, thank God."

3. Or perhaps you are thinking: "I don't know which of those two things I ought to think, but I think it is going to have to be one or the other." If so, that is at least the first either/or: the either/or between either/or (thing #1) and no either/or (thing #2). So two out of these three possible reactions move you at least a little bit, and with uncertainty, in one direction, while the other one moves you certainly and non-negotiably in the other. Well, as they say, two out of three ain't bad. And as they say in chess, it's your move now.

Your friend,
Peter Kreeft